Tage Frid Teaches Woodworking

Book I—Joinery

SO-AVG-837

Tage Frid Teaches Woodworking

Book 1 — Joinery

The Taunton Press

© 1979 by The Taunton Press, Inc.
Photographs and illustrations © 1979
by The Taunton Press, Inc.
All rights reserved

First Printing: 1979
International Standard Book Number 0-918804-03-5 (Hardcover)
International Standard Book Number 0-918804-04-3 (Softcover)
Library of Congress Catalog Card Number 78-65178
Printed in the United States of America

Fine Woodworking® is a trademark of The Taunton Press, Inc.,
registered in the U.S. Patent and Trademark Office.

The Taunton Press, Inc.
52 Church Hill Road
Box 355
Newtown, Connecticut 06470

Acknowledgments

My original agreement with the Taunton Press was to write three woodworking books in 1½ years, which I was sure I could do. Now, two years later, book one is finally finished. I had no idea how much work goes into writing a book and neither did Rosanne Somerson, who took most of the photographs and typed the whole manuscript from tapes, which was certainly not easy, if you have ever heard me talk. But being one of my former students, she managed. A special thanks to her for her great help.

I also want to thank Hank Gilpin for reading the first galley and offering many useful suggestions, and Roger Birn for taking some of the pictures.

If it had not been for my wife, this book would never have been written. Before Fine Woodworking *was established, the publisher, Paul Roman, asked me to write some articles. I was not interested at all. Never having written an article before, I felt I was not qualified, but my wife finally talked me into it. In thanks to her, I dedicate this book to my wife, Emma.*

Contents

Foreword

In 1977, a little more than a year after Tage Frid began writing articles as contributing editor to Fine Woodworking *magazine, it became apparent that those articles would make only an insignificant dent in the vast woodworking knowledge Frid had accumulated in his 50 years of cabinetmaking.*

Frid learned cabinetmaking as an apprentice in his native Denmark, a country long noted for its strong woodworking tradition. After World War II, the American Crafts Council asked Frid to transfer some of this lore by establishing a woodworking program at the School for American Craftsmen, which was then at Alfred University but soon to be at Rochester Institute of Technology, where it remains today.

Frid set up the program and stayed 14 years at RIT until 1962, when he joined the faculty at the Rhode Island School of Design as professor of woodworking and furniture design, a position he still holds.

Over the years, Frid has taught a multitude of students to be well-versed in the many ways of working wood. Check the furniture conservation and restoration departments of major American museums, or the faculty of college-level woodworking and furniture-design programs in this country, and likely as not you'll find a former Frid student. And of course, many other students have become commercially successful woodworkers.

The Frid hallmark is to teach virtually all the techniques and tools available to the woodworker. Thus his students are able to tackle any woodworking assignment under any shop conditions. This approach is also crucial to furniture design, where Frid's motto is to design around the construction. When one knows all the ways of making furniture, one also knows how to design furniture without falling into the trap of designing a piece that cannot be successfully made.

Frid's students come out of his courses able to design and build furniture in any style, though most naturally prefer the contemporary idiom, as does Frid. But even here, Frid encourages students to go their own way in design—so much so that it's impossible to tell what Frid's own design style is by looking at the work of his pupils.

Frid also believes his students should know how to make a living from working with wood, so he stresses the production techniques individual designer-craftsmen will need to know if they are to turn out work that is both well designed and efficiently produced—in other words, work that is many cuts above mass-produced furniture, but still competitively priced.

Frid himself has kept in touch with the commercial aspects of woodworking by accepting a string of commissions that range from kitchen cabinets to corporate boardrooms to church interiors, as well as difficult restorations like the 19th-century ship interiors at Mystic (Conn.) Seaport. And just this year, the Boston Museum of Fine Arts commissioned Frid to create some public seating that will become part of its permanent collection.

As his former students and clients can easily attest, Frid has much to teach, and thus we decided to do a series of three books on everything Frid knows about woodworking, structured in the same way as the courses he has taught. The first book would be about joinery and tools, for that's where woodworking must begin; the second about bending, turning, shaping, veneering and otherwise working with wood. The third volume would put these techniques all together into one book on the design and construction of furniture.

Frid's woodworking shop behind his farmhouse in Foster, Rhode Island, was converted to a photo studio. A former student, Rosanne Somerson, signed on for a time as scribe, editor and photographer. And Frid's wife, Emma, kept things organized and flowing smoothly. This first volume is the result, and the other two should be ready in the next couple of years.

This book has been organized around processes, and it has been designed more as a shop manual than as a text or craft book. Each page or spread is self-contained—the text accompanying pictures is usually right alongside the pertinent pictures. Boldface numbers set into the text refer to the appropriate illustration. Where necessary, cross references to other parts of the book are included.

Short sections devoted to jigs, tips or particular tools are set off from the rest of the text by a light grey background. Those sections dealing with cutting joints usually end with a series of sequential drawings that recap the cutting of the joint. The color in each drawing highlights the cut being made at that time. The result is shown in black in subsequent drawings.

Because each section deals with a single subject, the table of contents also serves as an index.

A word about the photos: Most were taken in Frid's own shop. In the interest of clarity, safety guards were sometimes removed from machines, and scribed lines were sometimes darkened with a pencil.

This book is intended for the woodworker who wishes to learn how to select the best joints for the job at hand, and how to lay them out and cut them more accurately and efficiently. Novices will be able to follow Frid's step-by-step instructions; intermediates will improve their techniques and certainly pick up many tips; advanced woodworkers will be challenged by the more difficult joinery.

Newtown, Conn.
July 28, 1979

Paul Roman, Editor-in-Chief
The Taunton Press

Introduction
Chapter 1

This book is intended for small professional shops, schools and hobbyists. There are many ways to do some of the things I have described, and these are the ways that I have found to be the easiest and best through many years of experimenting. I have taught many of the woodworkers in this country who are now teachers, as well as many of the individual craftsmen. Most of them still use the methods that I taught them.

Many woodworking books have information that I find unnecessary. If I didn't need that information in the 50 years that I have been working with wood, I am sure that you won't either. There will be no charts for nail and screw sizes, sandpaper grits and the like. No industrial production machines will be covered. But each technique and every joint will be explained and demonstrated. I will describe how to perform various operations by hand, using small electric hand tools, and the small machines that a craftsman or hobbyist is likely to have access to. Each tool, material and machine will be introduced as it is needed to accomplish a specific operation.

You may notice that some of the machinery and tools in the photographs look worn and old. In many cases they are. I have had a good working relationship with all of these tools for many years; and I wouldn't feel right about ignoring this relationship by buying shiny new tools just for the photographs. You may have tools that you feel this way about now. If not, assuming that you care for your tools, you probably will someday. I will not go into too great detail about all the adjustments on the machines, because machines vary so much from brand to brand. But special tricks for operating them will be covered.

Most of what is in this book, I learned from older craftsmen when I was young. They, of course, were taught by some other craftsmen, so the trade has been passed on from generation to generation. A few things in this book I feel I have improved on, but the foundation is still what I learned when I was young. One thing I can't stand is when people who went through the same learning as I, won't pass it on to the younger generation. They keep it a secret as if it belonged only to them and seem to forget that they learned it from someone else.

The purpose of this book is to help you do things right. The easiest thing in the world is to make mistakes. The difficult thing is to know how to get out of those mistakes. In many instances you can't afford to throw out the piece with the mistake on it. You might be working on something where you have carefully matched the grain. Or you might be working with a special wood that is scarce and expensive. As well as teaching you how to do a certain technique, I will try in many cases to tell you what to do if you make a mistake.

I hope you will enjoy this book and learn enough to make beautiful, lasting pieces of furniture.

Some thoughts on being a woodworker I have chosen to be a designer-craftsman. Most of my life I have concentrated on designing and working only with wood, and, having spent more than 50 years with that one material, I am still learning through experimentation and looking for new techniques and forms.

The only trouble with designing and working in wood is that it has the advantage — or disadvantage, however you look at it — of being beautiful in itself. It is not like metal. A piece of metal by itself is very cold and has to be hammered, shaped and polished before people will even look at it. A piece of clay, which is really dirt, must be shaped, fired and glazed. But take a piece of wood — plane, sand and oil it, and you will find it is a beautiful thing. The more you do to it from then on, the more chance that you will make it worse. Therefore, working with a material of such natural beauty, I feel that we have to design very quietly and use simple forms.

On being an apprentice I was born in Denmark, so therefore my background for furniture is a little different from that of most American furniture designers. That may be the reason that I view design from a slightly different angle and feel strongly about the background that a furniture designer should have. I started as an apprentice in a cabinetmaker's shop in Copenhagen when I was very young. Because I was not what you would call an outstanding student in school, I decided that the best thing for me to do was to serve an apprenticeship.

When you become an apprentice in Denmark, you sign a five-year contract, which is binding on both parties. Those were five of the longest years that I have ever spent! The working hours were from 7 AM to 5 PM, and I was required to attend technical school at night, where drawing and a knowledge of the materials were taught. The salary was one dollar a week and the guarantee that I would be a journeyman at the end of five years. I did not learn very much about design, but I did learn a good deal about wood as a material — its strength, its limitations and how it is put together.

In many ways I still think the apprenticeship system is one of the best ways to learn about a material and the craft of working with it, but it is just about impossible to get a situation like that here. In Europe, craftsmen enjoy the recognition they deserve. Here, an effort should be made to put more respect into vocational training. A student taking vocational training may be just as intelligent as a student enrolled in a college program. The only difference is that the student has a different goal. I think it is better to be a good craftsman and happy than to be a doctor or lawyer and unhappy just to satisfy mom and dad.

I think we have to start with the teachers of vocational subjects in high schools by giving them a better background. Instead of teaching them a little of each craft and having them become jacks-of-all-trades, they should be taught one craft so that when it is mastered they can teach students in that particular field. I think also that they should be furnished with a better design background themselves in order to be able to guide the students in making their own designs. Now, a student who wants to make a coffee table is told to go to drawer #3 and pick a design, usually from some popular magazine, which certainly does not help the student to understand good design. A vocational student should be instructed in design and art history, as well as mechanical drawing, materials and processes.

Educators today like to talk about the spiral where the student knows a little bit about everything before finally reaching perfection. I think it would be much better to turn the spiral upside-down and learn one thing well, and, as you go on and improve, spread yourself out to other fields. However, I believe students should make up their mind at an early point what their major will be and spend much more time in it. I'm afraid the present educational system, where the students spend a few hours in one field and the next few hours in another, leads only to confusion, and they are unable to decide what they really want to do.

Knowledge of materials   In 1948 I started teaching in the School for American Craftsmen, now located in Rochester, N.Y. When I arrived at the school, the students and some of the teachers kept talking about the "freedom of the material." This sounded interesting to me, and I could hardly wait to find out what it was all about. It didn't take me very long to find out when I started teaching. They did not have control of the material, so many of the things made were actually accidents.

I do not think that all furniture designers should be craftsmen first, but I certainly am convinced that designers should know the material in which they are going to design. I really do not see how designers can go in cold and design something in a material about which they have no knowledge. Even for a professional, it is extremely difficult to switch from one material to another and do a good job.

Design and construction   If you combine technique and knowledge of the material, you certainly should be able to design and make some interesting and beautiful furniture, because if you have this background, you will automatically design around the construction, and not construct around the design. You will combine technique and form when you are designing—as construction becomes second nature. I am sorry to say that many times a different approach is used—that is, to construct around the design. Many designers are so worried about the looks and the sculptural qualities of the piece that they first think about the beauty of the piece and later worry about how it is put together. I strongly believe that this is the wrong approach to take when you are designing furniture. When people buy furniture, they are very practical—they want a chair they can sit on and a bed they can sleep in. Customers may, for example, buy a sterling-silver coffeepot that will tarnish and be unsafe to use to show that they can afford expensive items, or for whatever personal reason. They may buy a vase for its beauty even though it may have a crack in it. But when they are buying furniture, they want something they can use.

Furniture I feel that a piece of furniture should be in proportion to the size of the buyer and reflect his or her own personality. I don't think that anything can make a small person look more ridiculous—and perhaps make him feel smaller—than disappearing into an oversized, upholstered chair; or the reverse of a large person sitting on a delicate chair in which the chair disappears, and the person seems to be sitting on four legs. Furniture should be proportioned to the person who uses it. For example, there are certain requirements a chair must have. It should be designed so that it looks inviting to sit on, you should be able to sit in various positions, and it should be able to take the sitter's weight under stress circumstances. A chair is difficult to design because it has to fit the contours of the body, which haven't changed much since people started sitting on chairs. At the same time, a chair has to look good from all angles.

The furniture I have been talking about is the more functional type. There are others, for instance, the type that you are supposed to "discover," where the sculpture of the piece becomes more important than the function. A few designers and craftsmen can make this type, but one could not start an industry based on it. A designer-craftsman would have to design and make it because it would be so personalized that it would be impossible to make a working drawing, or to get anyone else to make it. But it would be very refreshing to have a few pieces of this furniture in your home. A limited number would be fine, because I don't want to spend half of my time trying to discover where I am going to sit in my own home. I am in favor of individual furniture, make it quite often myself and encourage my students to do so. It is fun to make a piece of sculpture that you can also sit on.

Designer-craftsmen If you study the older furniture designers, you will find that they were craftsmen, and they all designed around the construction. For that reason, we still enjoy their furniture today, and it mixes very well with well-designed contemporary furniture. The good furniture designer of today uses the same techniques, and those pieces will later become classical furniture. But in many cases the designs are copies, and to cut costs, shortcuts are taken. This is why we have some of the miscarriages we see today. Of course, I am fully aware that the high cost of material and labor and the shortage of skilled labor have a big influence on today's designs. But I still don't believe an inexpensive piece of furniture has to look cheap. The disappearance of the designer-craftsman was one of the prices we had to pay here in America for having mass production. In Europe they are specializing also, and the decline in the crafts field is noticeable, too. But it does not mean that it is dying. We don't need as many craftsmen as we once had because we have machines.

Many people think that the craftsman makes everything by hand. He does not, of course. He takes advantage of all the machines and techniques that are available. Some people think it is wonderful that something is made "by hand." I don't care how it is made—he can make it with his teeth or a machine—it is still the final product that counts. A craftsman is very flexible and it does not cost much to switch from one design to another; therefore he is able to combine machine work and handwork to get more individual pieces. Even in a small production line, each piece can still have its own individuality. I think a designer-craftsman can compete in price with factory-made furniture because people usually go directly to him, and the dealer's in-between costs are cut. The craftsman can customize the furniture to fit the customer's taste. He can alter a piece of furniture, making it slightly larger or smaller to fit in a particular place without having to increase the cost. Without the tremendous overhead the factory carries, the price will be pretty close to what a factory-made piece of the same quality would cost. So I believe there is a great opportunity and a great need for designer-craftsmen today, and that most clients are looking for something with a more personal touch and of better quality than is available in stores. □

The Material
Chapter 2

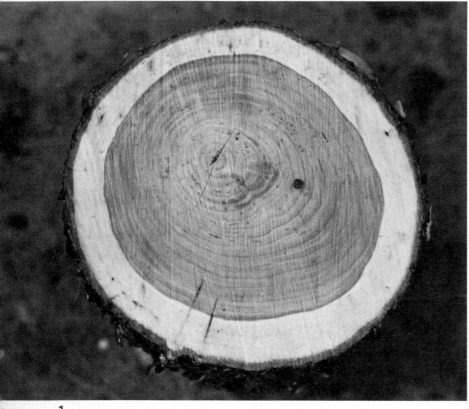

1

2

Wood

Trees A woodworker must have a basic understanding of the growth and structure of trees in order to design with an understanding of what can and cannot be done with wood. Only a few of the many trees that grow in this country and in other parts of the world ever reach the cabinetmaker in lumber form. Some woods warp and twist too much to be of practical use; others are too colorless or lack variety of grain; others are too soft. But all woods, regardless of their different characteristics, are subject to the stresses and strains inherent in their structure.

Wood is divided into two groups, hardwoods and softwoods. This has nothing to do with whether the wood is hard or soft—some softwoods are harder than hardwoods. The division into the two categories is by the type of leaves of the tree. Softwoods are generally evergreens, coniferous trees, and usually do not shed their leaves in the fall. Deciduous trees, which shed their leaves in the fall, make up the group of hardwoods.

Both the cell and the cell walls of a living tree are filled with moisture, or sap. When a tree is felled, the moisture in the cells, called free moisture, is the first to drain out or evaporate. Once the cells are free of moisture, the cell walls gradually give up the moisture that has soaked into them. It is this drying process that causes the stresses that result in warpage, twisting, checking and shrinking. This is true in all types of lumber. The moisture content of wood is of prime concern to anyone designing or constructing furniture and cannot be ignored.

Logs I don't think I have to explain about the birds and the bees. We all know that the seed gets into the ground and the sapling gets started and each year puts a new year ring on. A tree grows from the inside out, which means that the closer you get to the center, the older the wood.

(1) Let's examine the end of a cherry log after it is cut. Notice the dark heartwood and the light sapwood. Each year a new ring is added to the sapwood, and one sapwood year ring on the inside dies and gets added to the heartwood. The tree does not grow at the same rate during the year—it grows faster in the spring and slower in the summer. The faster spring growth is softer and lighter than the slower summer growth. And the tree does not grow the same size annual rings each year: It all depends on the weather.

(2) This log was plainsawn, or cut tangentially to the annual rings. The cut angles in to make the figure more apparent. Since the color differs from spring to summer growth, very beautiful and interesting patterns result. You can see how the grain of the sliced vertical section relates to the rings on the end.

Many times you hear people who have turned or carved a bowl saying, "I studied the grain before I started shaping the wood." This is a good sales pitch, but it is a lot of baloney. When you carve or turn a bowl the rings follow the shape as you cut through them. But you can control the figure by the way you orient the bowl. In drawing **(3)**, the graining will be very strong with the annual rings cut at a great angle. If the bowl is oriented in the opposite direction **(4)**, the rings will be cut at about 90°, making the graining of the bowl straight.

(5) This log has a quartersawn section removed. Cutting perpendicular to the annual rings gives a straight grain. If used right, straight grain can be quite effective visually. Quartersawn lumber is best suited to lamination and steam-bending.

(6) This log is cut right through the heartwood. The center of the log can't be used but the pieces to either side of the center are usable. There the graining is straight as in quartersawn lumber.

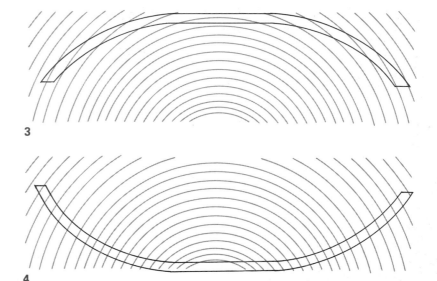

3

4

5

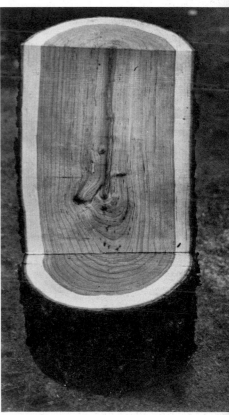

6

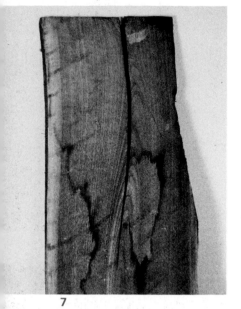

7

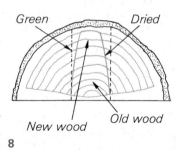

Green   Dried

New wood   Old wood

8

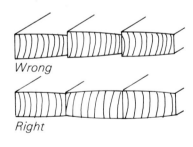

Wrong

Right

9

(7) The pith, or center of the log, can't be used, because it will crack when it is dry.

Drying As soon as wood is sawn, drying becomes a problem. Whether it will be air-dried or kiln-dried, wood should be kept out of the sun and properly stacked. If planks of wet lumber are piled on top of each other, with no space between them, the lumber will soon discolor and begin to rot.

For air-drying, the boards must be kept off the ground, and sometimes it's advisable to coat the ends with hot paraffin or paint to prevent too rapid drying. The sticks they rest on to keep them off the ground have to be leveled off. Between each layer of wood, sticks of even thickness (about ¾ in. square) should be placed directly over each other for even air circulation. The top of the pile should be covered. If kept inside, they should be stored in an open shed to allow air circulation. To check for dryness, keep some pieces 3 ft. to 4 ft. long on the outside of the pile, about halfway up. Weigh them every month and put a date on them each time. When the weight stabilizes, all the wood should be fairly dry.

Exactly how wood moves depends on how the board was cut and from what part of the tree it came.

We know that the center of the tree is the oldest and the outside the youngest **(8)**, which means the pores or cells on the outside are more open than the center ones, so the outside will shrink more than the inside. This tells how the wood moves after it is cut and dried.

The reason that this is important is that after the wood is dried and made into a piece of furniture, the wood will continue to expand and shrink across both the grain and the thickness every year with the seasons. How much it moves depends on how dry our houses get in winter, and how damp in summer, and on the type of wood.

Just as the new, outside wood shrinks more when it dries, so it expands more when the humidity rises. This means that when joining boards together — say, for a tabletop, or whatever — the boards should be chosen and placed such that new wood should be joined to new wood, old wood to old wood **(9)**. Otherwise, no matter how well you plane and sand the boards after joining them, the different rates of expansion and contraction will guarantee an uneven joint as soon as the humidity changes.

Storing and buying lumber Storing lumber is often a problem, because it occupies too much space in the shop, even if it is stored in a rack. Many times the lumber has to be stored someplace else, in my case in my barn. Usually the barn is more humid than the shop, so I bring the lumber I am going to use for a specific job into the shop a couple of weeks ahead of time. I buy my lumber in the rough from different lumberyards, and prefer to select it myself. It is more expensive, but I can select the pieces for color, width, etc., so there is less waste. I would never buy lumber that is jointed and thickness-planed, because it would warp badly before I got it made into furniture. If I didn't have a jointer and thickness-planer (and didn't want to mill it by hand) I would still buy it rough and get it jointed and planed locally just before I was ready to use it. When using solid wood it is important to work as fast as possible, from the time the wood is cut, jointed and planed until all the joints are made. Storing the wood while the joints are being made is very important. Either leave it so the air can circulate around it or stack it so no air can get to it. Never leave a piece of wood overnight with one side covered and the other side exposed to the air, because it will definitely cup or warp in some direction.

I don't feel it is necessary to use exotic wood to make good furniture. The wood I like and work most with is what grows in my own back yard, such as maple, cherry and walnut. I feel I would be a bad designer if I could not make and design furniture out of that material.   □

Designing with Wood

Before designing and/or making a piece of furniture, one must know the characteristics of the material that is going to be worked. With wood, one has to understand how it moves, twists, shrinks and warps, and how it can and cannot be joined together. **(1)** Wood can be glued together long grain to long grain.

(2,3,4) The direction of the grain is not that important as long as the joint is long grain to long grain.

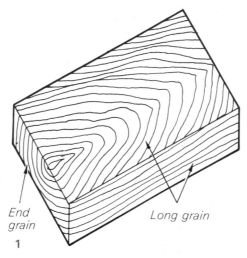

End grain

Long grain

1

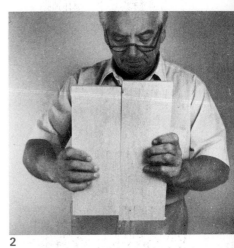

2

4

3

5

8

6

9

7

10

11

(5) We cannot glue end grain to end grain. Nor can we glue end grain to long grain **(6,7)** as is necessary in carcase construction, say, in making a chest, drawers or a box. So when joining two pieces end grain to long grain, we have to choose a joint that will give as much long-grain to long-grain contact as possible. End grain does not count as a glue surface in any joint. My advice is that if you are learning carcase construction and you begin by making, say, a hope chest, make it for small hopes. You will learn as much making a small piece as you will a larger piece, and you will save time and expense, especially if you make a mistake.

In frame construction, we join the width of the wood to the edge of the board **(8)**. This type of construction is used for doors, windows, chairs, tables and the like. Again, unless there is a good joint, one cannot glue long grain to end grain. When choosing a joint for the piece you are going to make, there is usually no doubt which type of construction you are going to use, it is either carcase or frame.

If a piece of wood is cut across the grain, so that there is barely any length of long grain **(9,10,11)**, the piece will break easily. These short sections of long grain are referred to as "short grain" and should never be used.   □

Saws
Chapter 3

1

2

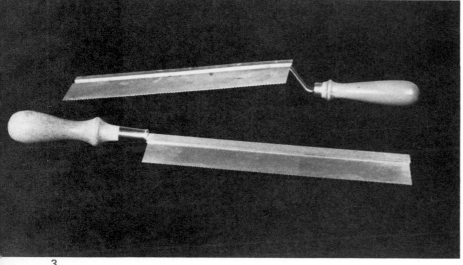

3

Choosing Handsaws

Regardless of how many power saws you have in your shop, there are a number of handsaws you should also have. Of course a handsaw is one of the most difficult tools to learn to use correctly, but it is also an extremely important tool for woodworking, because it can replace a machine-powered saw for every cutting operation. After you have learned to control a saw, it will become easy to cut square and rip accurately, and to make joints that fit the first time.

There are many handsaws on the market, and each one is designed for a special purpose. The **(1)** bowsaw, **(2)** scroll bowsaw, **(3)** offset dovetail saw (top), straight dovetail saw (bottom) and **(4)** rip panel saw are the saws I have found most useful in my many years of cabinetmaking. I would never buy a backsaw; they are clumsy and heavy. Maybe they are all right in miter boxes, but a bowsaw will do the job faster.

On these bowsaws, the tensioning system is twisted wire attached on one end to a threaded eyebolt with a wing nut. The more common tensioning system uses a string instead of wire (see p. 17).

For general sawing, I would recommend buying a 26-in., 6-point and an 18-in., 8-point bowsaw. (Handsaws are sold by length and by points, or teeth per inch—a 6-point saw has six teeth per inch. Lengths might vary slightly, because most bowsaws are made in Europe and so are measured in metrics.) I would also buy a 26-in. scroll bowsaw, preferably with interchangeable blades, and a 10-in. or longer 15-point off-set dovetail saw. A 24-in. 6 to 7-point rip panel saw (the standard carpenter's saw) is useful for cutting big pieces such as plywood, where the bridge of the bowsaw would be in the way.

Japanese saws **(5)** are good for special work. I have some but hardly ever use them, except in cramped spaces where I can't get in with a regular saw. The Japanese ripsaw cuts on the pull stroke—not the normal push stroke—which makes the line fuzzy and hard to see when cutting joints the Western way. The Japanese crosscut saw **(6)** has long teeth that might bend when hitting a knot. It's also difficult to resharpen, even with special files.   □

4

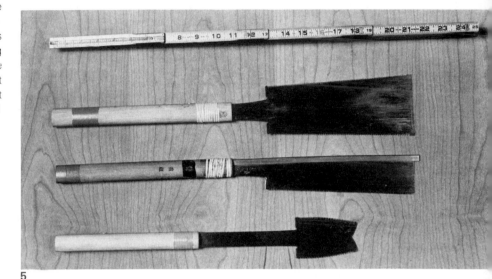

5

6

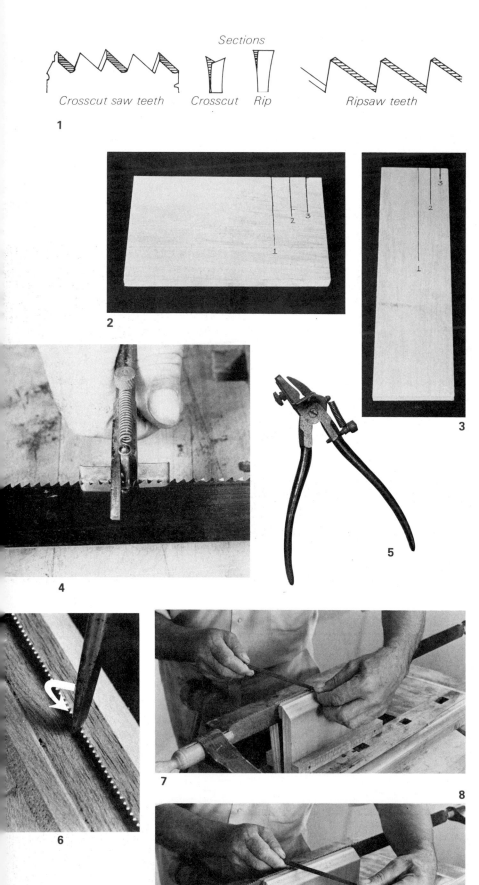

Sections

Crosscut saw teeth   Crosscut   Rip   Ripsaw teeth

1

2

3

4

5

6

7

8

Sharpening Handsaws

Woodworkers should know how to sharpen their tools, because most tools don't arrive from the factory sharpened right. Most new handsaws are filed for crosscutting, especially panel saws, which are used mostly by carpenters who do very little ripping and usually work in wet soft-wood. I generally use only dry hardwoods in my work.

The first time I sharpen a crosscut saw I change it to a ripsaw by changing the teeth from a point to a chisel edge **(1)**. This makes ripping faster and easier because there are more teeth per inch than would normally be available on a ripsaw, and I find the saw works better even for crosscutting. I usually demonstrate this to my new students because the difference in cutting speed is dramatic. I also use the same kind of demonstration to show that frame saws are much faster than panel saws for both ripping and crosscutting.

What's fastest? In both crosscutting **(2)** and ripping **(3)**, the ripsaw-sharpened bowsaw (cut 1) performs best. The ripsaw-sharpened panel saw (cut 2) is an improvement over the same saw with a crosscut sharpening (cut 3). The wood shown here is poplar.

All handsaws have an alternating tooth setting **(4)**, that is, the upper part of each tooth is bent out to one side or the other to create a kerf (the width of the sawcut) that is wider than the thickness of the sawblade. If the saw is not set enough, it will bind as it cuts. If it is set too much, the cut will be wide and rough and the saw will cut more slowly. If the teeth are set more to one side, the saw will favor that side. To correct this, both sides must be reset. A properly set saw that is started correctly without too much pressure will easily follow the cutting line. There are many good saw sets **(5)** on the market and you should follow their directions for use. I prefer the Sandvik, because it is light, easy to adjust and simple to use. It allows you to see what you are doing. Each tooth should be set approximately $\frac{1}{64}$ in. to each side.

If the teeth are too small to use a saw set (as on dovetail saws), use a small screwdriver instead to push the teeth out.

(6) Press the screwdriver down between every second tooth and twist it to set the teeth. Be sure to twist an equal amount each time. This takes practice.

Once the teeth are set they are ready to be filed. Use a new triangular file or an unused edge each time you file a saw. I never use an old, worn-out file. Using a file more than once will not do the job as well, and you may get uneven results. Use only one edge for each filing. By using the same number of strokes, the same length of each stroke (using your fingers or tape as a guide) and the same amount of pressure, all the teeth will be sharpened identically. The file gradually gets dull, but so gradually that all the teeth are the same length. Don't turn the file to a new edge in the middle of a sharpening—the new side will cut deeper than the worn one. This way the teeth stay the same length and you shouldn't have to level them off for many years.

When filing **(7,8)**, press straight down on the file, just enough so the file works and doesn't skip over the metal. File both the front and the back of the teeth at the same time, working from the front of the blade toward the handle of the saw. The final file stroke on each tooth will then be on the back **(9)**, and the burr that appears when the tooth just comes to a point will be aimed in the cutting direction. Be sure to keep the file strokes at a 90° angle to the blade. Don't file the teeth of a ripsaw from alternate sides, as many books recommend. It is not necessary. Never file or stone the face of the blade, because this will change the set of the teeth.

The saw can be refiled four or five times before it needs resetting. Of course this depends on how dull you let the saw get before you refile it. I always file my saws as soon as the ends of the teeth get shiny white **(10)**. This means the saw has started to get dull. If the saw isn't too dull, two file strokes on each tooth should be enough to resharpen it.

If the wood tears up at the back when crosscutting or ripping, one or more of the teeth are too long. In this case I file across the top of the teeth **(11)** with a flat mill file to even the length of the teeth. Push the file along the length of the blade.

When all the teeth are the same height **(12)**, refile the teeth with the triangular file until they all come to a point **(13)**. Then reset, and refile as usual.

If the teeth still tear after resharpening, as is likely to happen in softwoods and especially in plywood **(14)**, scribe a line where the cut will be and **(15)** make a V-cut with a chisel on the underside of the piece **(16)**. This will prevent tearing. □

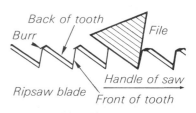
9

10

11

12

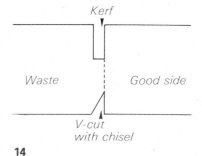
14

13   15   16

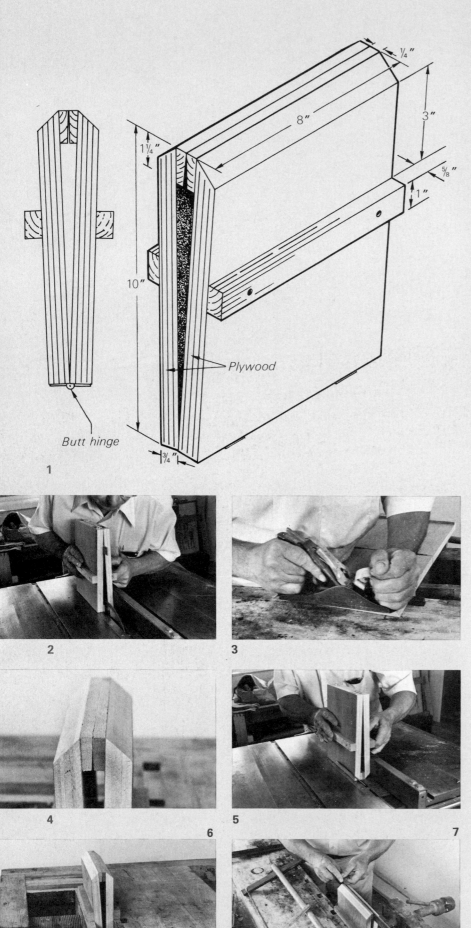

Plywood

Butt hinge

1

2

3

4

5

6

7

Making a Sharpening Vise

Vises to hold saws for sharpening are commercially available, but I prefer to make my own. The one shown here **(1)** requires two pieces of ¾-in. plywood, four strips of hardwood (such as maple), four screws and two butt hinges (with accompanying screws).

Glue the two pieces of hardwood on the ends of the plywood. These will be the jaws for the jig. Once the glue sets, attach the two halves at the other end (which will be the bottom) with the butt hinges. Glue and screw on the other two strips of wood on the outside. These prevent the jig from falling through the bench vise.

Make the jaws parallel using a table saw **(2)** or plane **(3)**. If you use a table saw, insert a thin strip of wood between the two plywood pieces to prevent the jaws from binding on the sawblade at the end of the cut.

To make it possible to use the full length of the file, bevel both jaw ends 45° **(4)**, using either a table saw **(5)** or a hand plane.

(6) The sharpening jig sits in the bench vise and **(7)** holds the sawblade securely. You can change the dimensions of the jig to suit your particular needs. □

Using Handsaws

(1) The bowsaw is my all-purpose saw. It takes longer to learn to use than other handsaws, but once you get the hang of it, you will use it for most cutting. All my advanced students use a bowsaw, and I don't brainwash my students. It has several advantages. Because the blade is narrower and thinner than other saws, there is less friction in the kerf. The blade does not whip because it is kept in tension. Because the steel is thinner than in a panel saw, the bowsaw advances more quickly, and it is easier to cut a straight line.

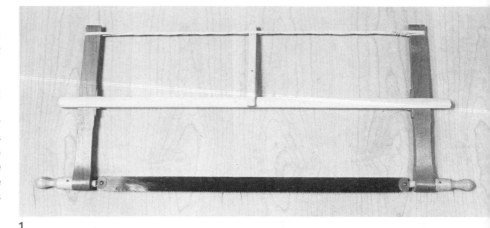

1

When you buy a bowsaw that uses string as a tensioning system (which I prefer), you usually get the saw in pieces. Even if it comes assembled, you must know how to string it in case the string breaks. I use common chalk line. Clamp the saw in the bench so that there is just a slight amount of tension in the blade. After wrapping the string lengthwise, wind it around six times **(2)**. Then finish stringing by weaving the end in and out of the strings about four times. Then place the pin, the short piece of wood that controls the blade tension, between the strings. Release the tension when the saw is not in use.

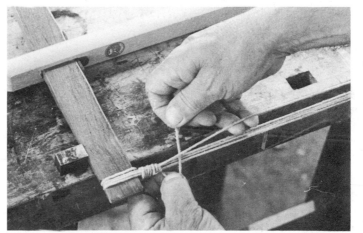

2

3

When the bowsaw is assembled and tightened, look down the blade **(3)** to be sure it isn't twisted.

The blade need not be parallel to the frame. It can also be angled **(4)** to make cuts beyond the depth of the bridge.

The correct use and maintenance of handsaws should be practiced until they are second nature. To saw properly **(5)**, coordination of the joints in the hand, elbow and shoulder must be achieved. The biggest mistake most people make when using a handsaw is to hang onto it as if their lives depended on it, bearing down much too hard. This makes it hard to start the cut, and once the cut is started, it is hard to follow the line. A handsaw should lie loosely in your hands. No pressure should be applied after the cut is started.

(6) Use your thumb as a guide to start the saw.

4

5

6

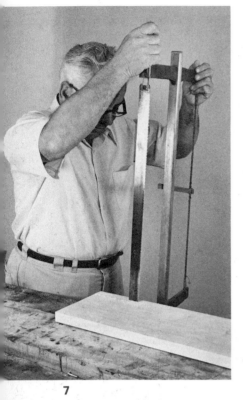

7

8

9

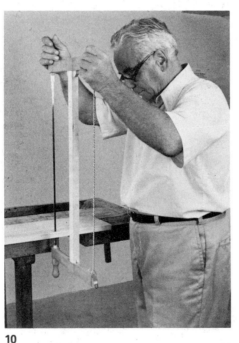

10

When I rip with a bowsaw I clamp the board down on the bench and cut vertically **(7,8)**. I can cut faster this way because I am sawing up and down and can put more force into the downstroke. I use both hands so I don't tire easily. Also, by clamping the board with the portion to be ripped extended over the edge of the bench, I have to clamp the board only once. If I stood the board up in the vise, I would have to keep clamping and unclamping to reposition it as I cut. I am also able to rip long boards (say, 8 ft.) this way without a ladder and without the board vibrating. When I rip with a bowsaw, I hold it so the blade is 90° to the board. All the force is from the right hand, with the left hand acting as a guide. I saw away from myself so that I can see the line, and so that I can move along with the cut, with my arms in a comfortable position.

For crosscutting I use a rip bowsaw. I lay the board flat on the bench **(9)**, with the piece I am cutting extending to my right off the bench. I start by holding the wood down with my left hand. Then, when the wood is almost cut through, I plant my left elbow on the board to hold it and reach between the blade and the bridge of the saw to catch the cutoff so it doesn't splinter.

For scroll work, I would of course use a band saw if I could. Or I might use a sabre saw. But a scroll bowsaw **(10)** will cut just as fast or faster than a sabre saw, and no electricity is needed. The blade on the scroll bowsaw is considerably longer than that of any other scroll saw or coping saw. The $\frac{3}{8}$-in. blade is the easiest to get in this country. In Europe, you could get as small as $\frac{1}{8}$ in. and as large as $\frac{1}{2}$ in.

For very small work I use an offset dovetail saw **(11)**. With the offset, I can see the line I am sawing more easily and can use the saw for cutting anything that protrudes above a flat surface flush with that surface. I also change the dovetail saw from a crosscut to a rip the first time it needs filing. I don't like the reversible offset dovetail saw—it is very bulky, and because I change it to a ripsaw, I can use it only one way anyway. □

11

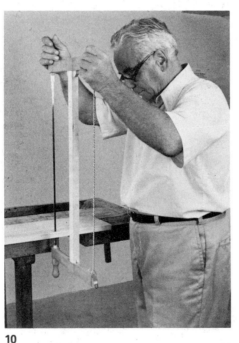

Circular Saws

Three types of circular saws are generally used in a small woodworking shop: the table saw **(1)**, the radial arm saw **(2)** and the portable circular saw **(3)**. In the table saw, the blade is stationary in a table and the wood is moved through the blade. In the radial arm saw the wood is stationary, and the blade is moved on an extended arm through the wood. In the portable circular saw, or contractor's saw, the saw is moved over a stationary piece of wood. This saw is more useful to the carpenter than to the cabinetmaker. It is less accurate and less flexible than the non-portable saws, but may be useful to the cabinetmaker for making inital cuts in plywood sheets that are too large for stationary saws. A 6-in. saw is adequate for a cabinetmaker, but a carpenter might want a larger blade.

Of the other two types of saws, my advice is to buy a table saw, not the radial arm. The latter is limited in function, much more difficult to use, less accurate for fine joinery or cutting, and cannot perform all the operations a table saw can. The radial arm saw was designed to cut rough lumber to length, but even there it is limited to a certain width. Many of the joints described in this book would be impractical, and even dangerous, to make on a radial arm saw.

Buy at least a 10-in. table saw, which costs only a little more than an 8-in. saw. Get at least a 1-hp motor—2 hp is even better. Make sure the arbor tilts for making angled cuts. Tilting the top is awkward. I find extension rails on the side helpful for large pieces of wood. You'll find the table saw the most used piece of equipment in your shop, so don't stint on quality.

I use a split knife behind the blade to prevent the piece of wood that is being cut from binding on the blade. Most saw guards that come with circular saws are clumsy, heavy, and, I feel, often dangerous. The split knife pictured here **(4)** is considerably safer and more compact. The block of wood on the top prevents sawdust and chips of wood from being thrown at my face. Before using this safety guard in a school, check first with your safety inspector. Always wear safety glasses or (even better) a face mask when using a circular saw or any power machine. ☐

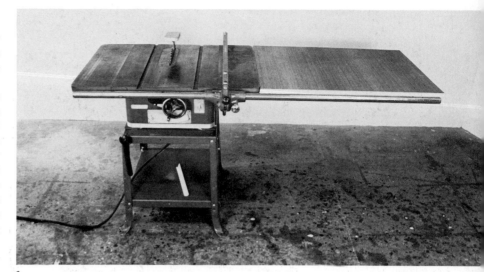

1

2

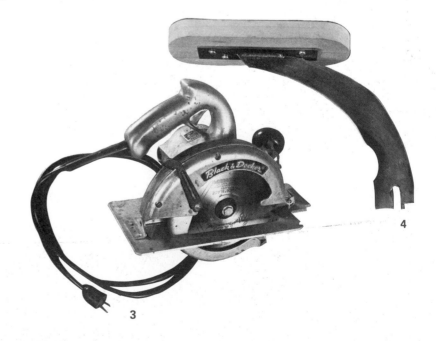

3

4

1

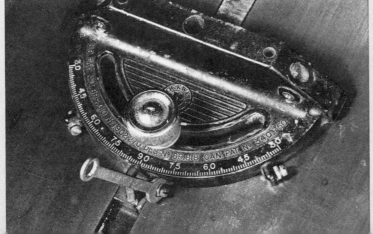

2

3

Miter Gauge

A miter gauge **(1)** fits into the grooves in the top of the saw table. Quite often the same miter gauge will fit into other machines such as band saws or disc sanders. It is used mostly in cutting the ends of boards either square or at angles. The smallest angle it can cut is 30°. A board screwed to the miter gauge gives it more stability.

(2) Three setscrews set (or calibrate) the gauge so it cuts accurately at 90° or 45° in both directions — the most used settings. When the gauge is set exactly, tighten the nuts **(3)** so the screws can't move. □

Circular-Saw Blades

There are many kinds of sawblades for special purposes. The craftsman who faces a production job may find that a special blade or cutter shortens the labor considerably, making it worthwhile to consult a saw manufacturer to find how much a custom-made blade would cost. Here I will discuss only those blades necessary for general shop work.

Circular-saw blades are available with or without carbide-tipped teeth. Blades without carbide tips must be sharpened and set quite often. I now use only carbide-tipped blades, except for very fine cutting, for which I use a hollow-ground blade, also called a planer blade.

(1) The three carbide-tipped blades I find most useful, in the order of their usefulness, are: a 40-tooth raker combination for roughing out; a 40-tooth blade for more precise work; and a 12-tooth rip for ripping. I also have a hollow-ground-planer that I use for very precise joinery. This is not carbide-tipped. Other non-carbide blades I have date back to earlier days, but I would not buy them new today. All my blades are 10 in., and in general, the more teeth, the finer the cut.

I have found that a carbide-tipped raker-tooth combination blade **(2)** is very useful for all-around work, including plywood, but not accurate enough for fine joinery. The teeth have a set because the carbide tips are not put all in a line **(3)**, as you can see from the photographs.

Of the carbide-tipped blades I have, I have found the 40-tooth blade with an 80° pitch **(4)** to be most accurate and cleanest cutting for my use, but it does have a tendency to tear a little in the back when crosscutting in soft woods. I also use it for precise cuts in plywood. If you are into mass production you should invest in a blade with more teeth.

The ripsaw blade **(5)** is used for cutting with the grain of the wood. It has teeth similar to those of a hand ripsaw — chisel sharpened and filed or ground to a right angle to the surface of the blade. The one I use is carbide-tipped, but if the blade is not, it should always be set, if necessary, before filing.

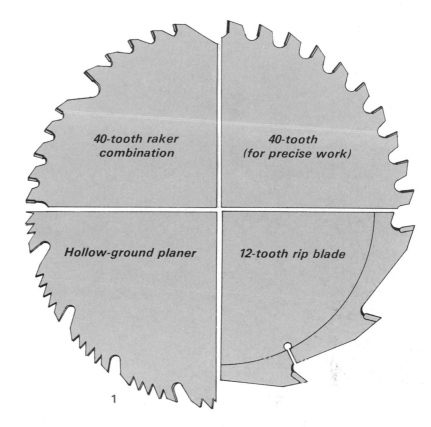

40-tooth raker combination

40-tooth (for precise work)

Hollow-ground planer

12-tooth rip blade

1

2

4

3

5

Hollow-ground blade section

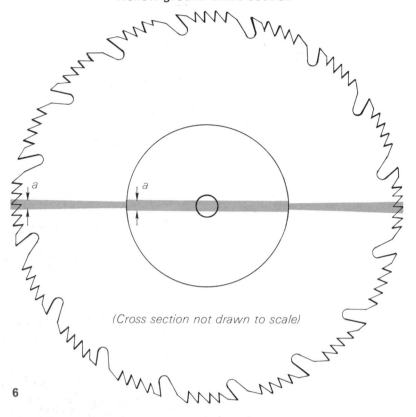

(Cross section not drawn to scale)

6

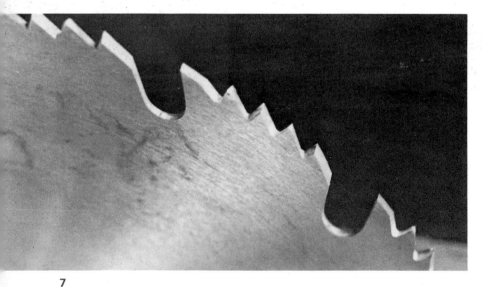

7

Carbide tips are welded to the steel teeth of the blade and given clearance by a bevel from front to back. These tips are exceedingly hard and brittle and must be handled with great care to prevent chipping or breaking. Never allow them to strike any hard or metallic surface.

Carbide-tipped blades are expensive and cannot be sharpened by the usual methods of saw sharpening. They should never be touched with a file or any ordinary grinding stone. Diamond honing stones may be used, but these are very expensive. Diamond grinding wheels suitable for machine grinding are much more so. It is usually better for the owner of a small shop to send carbide-tipped tools out to be sharpened.

The cutting teeth of all flat-ground blades must have some set in order not to bind in the wood. Blades that will be used to cut soft, wet lumber require more set than those to be used for hard, dry lumber. Only the outer third of the teeth should be bent out to the side, or set. In all cases, adjacent teeth should be set toward alternate sides of the blade.

A hollow-ground blade **(6)** is ground concave on both sides of the blade. This hollowing takes the place of the set necessary in flat-ground blades to prevent binding. Hollow-ground blades are never set. They are distinguished by the heavy hub around the arbor hole. On a new blade, this hub is the same thickness (or gauge) as the outer rim of the blade. The hollow grinding extends from near the hub to the circumference of the blade.

Hollow-ground blades give a very smooth cut and should be used for fine joinery rather than rough cutting. They are also good for ripping thin stock (less than ½ in.). Hollow-ground blades, more than any other type of blade, must be kept true and sharp at all times. Otherwise, because of the slight amount of clearance, they will heat up and burn. Photo **7** shows a hollow-ground blade; there is no setting.

The hollow-ground blade is a raker-tooth blade consisting of a group of cutting teeth accompanied by a chisel rip tooth, known as the raker or cleaner tooth. The cutting teeth are similar to crosscutting teeth and have similar bevels. The face of the cutting teeth are usually in line with the center of the blade. The raker teeth, however, have a different pitch. This pitch is best determined by making an outline drawing of the blade when it is new, so that when you file the blade you can check the pitch of the raker teeth with the drawing.

The raker teeth are filed exactly like the teeth of a ripsaw—square across the face and the back of the chisel edge. On crosscut and ripsaws of non-raker-tooth types, all the teeth should be the same length, and all should reach the outer diameter of the blade. But on the raker-tooth type, each of the raker teeth should be $\frac{1}{64}$ in. shorter than the cutting teeth. The cutting teeth, as the name indicates, do the cutting. The raker or cleaner teeth follow behind and chisel out the severed fibers in the saw kerf. If the wood tears up in the back when you cut with a raker-tooth blade, one or more of the raker teeth are too long. This happens only when the saw is not a carbide-tipped blade, and you can then file it yourself.

To find the tooth or teeth that are too long, turn the saw off and hold a piece of wood up to, but just barely clearing, the blade. Rotate the blade manually, checking which teeth hit the block of wood **(8)**. File any long teeth to the right length.

If after several filings, all the teeth have different lengths, the saw must be jointed, or in other words, the cutting circle of the teeth must be trued. This can be done with a stone held over the blade while the saw is running. For safety, the blade should be put on backwards, so that it runs in reverse. Otherwise, the teeth might pick up the stone and throw it back at you. Wear proper eye and face protection. Lower or raise the blade so that the points of the teeth barely touch a block of wood that is held down tightly over the throat of the table insert and passed over the blade with the machine off. Rotate the blade to make certain that the longer teeth barely touch the block.

Now take a grinding stone—an old one if

you have it—and with the saw running, move the stone along the table insert and across the points of the teeth **(9)**. Sparks will fly as the teeth touch the stone. It is better and safer to start with the teeth too low rather than too high, as the only purpose of this jointing operation is to grind off the points of the teeth that are too long and bring them down to the true circle. Move the stone over the revolving blade until no more sparks fly. Stop the saw and examine each of the teeth. Some may be considerably flatter than others; some may show a bright glitter only on the point. These shiny markings show where the stone has touched and whether all the teeth have been reduced to the cutting circle. If some have not been touched, raise the blade slightly and repeat the process. If there is a severe difference in the length of the teeth, I suggest sending the blade to a professional saw-sharpener.

If one or more cutting teeth in a raker blade are longer on one side of the blade than the other, the blade will wander toward that side. The blade will start binding, heating up and smoking. Here you can see that the teeth are longer on the right side **(10)**. To correct this, repeat exactly as when the raker teeth are too long.

Blades gum up if they are dull, if the wood is fed too slowly or when cutting pine or fir. Slow feeding heats up the blade and the heat causes gumming. If you continue to use the blade in this gummed condition, more heat will be generated and you will burn the wood. Even worse, the sawblade will get very hot and eventually blue, and the steel will lose its temper. The blade is no good after that. When my students continue to use a dull or gummed-up blade so that you can hardly see them for the smoke, I lose my temper, too.

A gummed-up sawblade is easy to clean. Pour some ammonia on the blade. Leave it for a few minutes, then scrub off the gum with steel wool. It comes off easily. Or you can brush on commercial oven-cleaner, let it sit for a few minutes, then rinse the blade. Or you can run it under hot water for several minutes, then use steel wool.   □

8

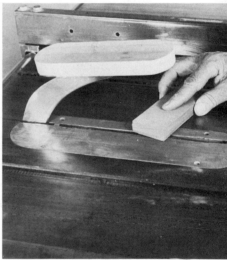

9

10

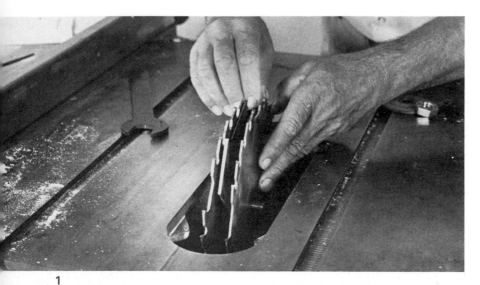

1

2

3

Dado Cutters

A dado head consists of two identical saw-blades with chisel-like spacer cutters in be-tween, all of exactly the same diameter. Each blade and spacer makes a ⅛-in. kerf (except one spacer that is only ¹⁄₁₆ in. thick). By using various combinations of blades and spacers, cuts of different widths can be made. If a small adjustment is needed, paper or metal shims can be inserted be-tween spacers. The chisel-like teeth of the spacers are swaged, so they overlap a bit and allow for these small adjustments. A dado can cut across or with the grain. It is useful for making straight grooves, as in drawers to hold the bottom. By tilting the blades you can make V-shaped grooves. **(1)** Always use a sawblade on both sides of the spacers.

(2) Never use one blade and one spacer unless you want to kill yourself. It doesn't matter how the spacers are spaced as long as the swaged tips don't interfere with each other or with the blades. Other dado heads on the market work in different ways, but I don't like them. I prefer the spacer type, which is much safer, easier to adjust, and does a better job of cutting if it is sharpened right, that is, with all the spacer cutters the same diameter as the sawblades. I wouldn't buy an adjustable dado (a one-piece unit) because it tends to kick back if forward pressure isn't maintained.

Dado blades are available with and without carbide tips. As with other blades, the car-bide-tipped ones cost more but cut well for a long time before they need sharpening. Blades sharpened as hollow-ground but not hollow-ground are cheaper, but need fre-quent sharpening. I feel they make a better cut. The main disadvantage is that they gum up easily.

When you use a dado blade, you usually need to make a wooden insert that fits flush with the table top. Make a piece the right thickness, size and shape, put on the dado head the width you will be cutting, and lower the dado blades below the table. **(3)** Put in the insert and clamp it in under a piece of wood in the back. Hold or clamp the front down. Slowly crank up the blade until it cuts a slot the size you need. (The double slots show that I use the wooden in-sert flipped over for other blades.) ☐

Circular-Saw Sharpening Jig

Most of my sawblades are carbide-tipped, and I send those out to be sharpened. I do sharpen the hollow-ground blades myself, and, being cheap, I still have a few very old blades that I also sharpen myself. It doesn't take very long. Several different jigs are commercially made to hold the saw while you file it. Most are quite expensive. I made my own and it works quite well. You need a piece of 2x4 hardwood about 18 in. long and two discs of ¾-in. thick plywood about 2 in. smaller in diameter than the blade to be sharpened **(1)**. Dish out the centers of the discs on a lathe or using a router **(2)**. This dishing out helps the outer edges hold the blade securely, especially when filing a hollow-ground blade **(3)**.

To use, clamp the blade in the jig **(4)** and proceed exactly as when filing a handsaw—(see p. 15) **(5,6,7)**. Loosen the wing nut and rotate the blade in the jig to get at all the teeth. For crosscut and hollow-ground blades, I file every other tooth and then reverse the blade and get the rest.

The same jig can be used to file a chain saw **(8)**. I prefer using it to filing the chain on the saw bar. If it is filed when still on the bar, some of the filings will fall into the grooves and act there as a grinding material. □

1

Disc scooped out on a lathe

Disc routed out

2

3

4

5

6

7

8

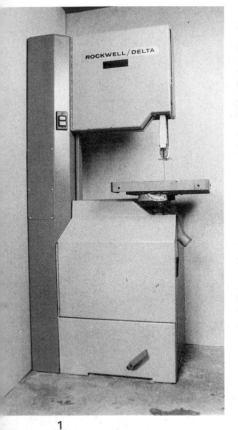

1

2

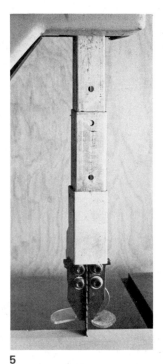

3   4   5

The Band Saw

Band saws are available in different sizes, such as 14 in., 16 in., 20 in., etc., which refers to the distance from the blade to the throat. The length and maximum width of the blade and the horsepower of the motor will correspond to the size of the throat. What size to buy depends on what kind of work you will do. If you are making instruments, a 14-in. band saw might be large enough, but for furniture buy at least a 20-in. band saw with a 2-hp motor — that's what I have.

The band saw (1) cuts curves and irregular shapes; it also resaws lumber. It has a continuous blade that is welded together and runs over two wheels (2). Usually the bottom wheel is powered and the top one is free. A guide above the table and one below help keep the blade tracking correctly. Blades of different widths can be used for different purposes. I prefer to use skiptooth blades. They cut faster, and the steel is harder so they last longer. They should be thrown out when they get dull. The maximum width of blade my band saw can take is 1 in., and the narrowest I use is 3/8 in. For most general work, I use a 1/2-in. or 3/4-in. blade.

A movable guard (3) covers the section of blade that is not needed to cut a particular thickness of wood. The greatest mistake most people make when cutting on the band saw is to cut a thick piece and then cut a thinner one without sliding down the guard (4). A large portion of the blade is thus exposed. If the blade breaks (as it sometimes does), dangerous pieces of the blade could fly all over. With the upper guard close to the wood (5), there is much more control over the blade, so the blade won't wander as easily.

There are different-style guides for the blade, depending on the manufacturer. The best guide is ball-bearing wheels on each side of the blade, but they are very expensive. I am satisfied with the guide that came with my band saw **(6)**, which does not have ball bearings. **(7)** Most band saws have a scale on them that will show the proper tension on the blade.

The upper guide should be not more than ½ in. above the piece being cut. This guides the blade better and lessens the risk of an exposed blade. If a blade does break, it usually makes a lot of noise. Don't open the door to see what happened. Wait until the machine has stopped running completely and is totally quiet. Then open the door, untangle the blade and replace it.

(8,9,10) Always keep your hands to the side of the blade or behind the blade, never in front of the blade.

6

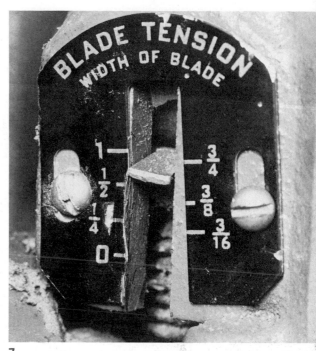

7

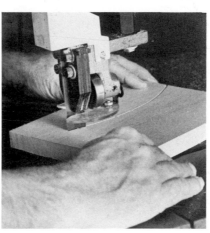

8

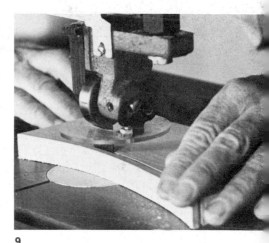

9

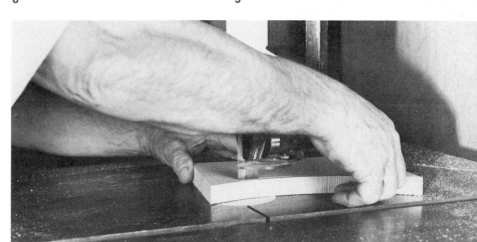

10

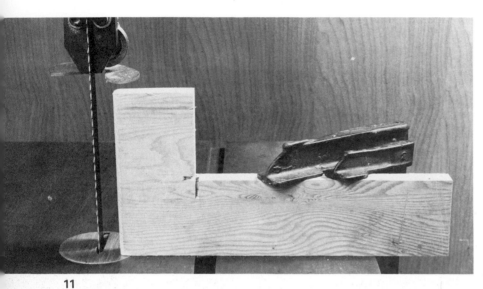

11

For resawing there is usually no fence available for smaller band saws. Because the blade always has a tendency to wander and favor one side or the other, a long fence won't work. Instead, I use a piece of ¾-in. plywood with the end square to the table as a guide **(11)**. Chamfer the edges nearest the sawblade. Rough-plane one side of the board to be resawn and square one edge. The square edge should be down toward the table. Draw a pencil line on top, follow the line free-hand and use the widest blade your band saw can handle **(12,13)**.   □

12

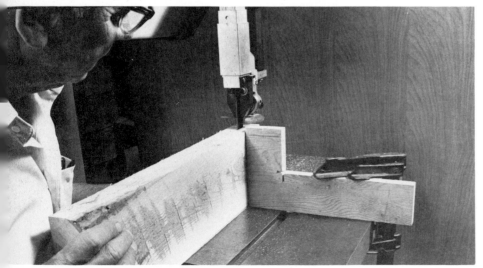

13

Handling a Band-Saw Blade

If you don't know how to unfold and fold a band-saw blade correctly, learn now because it is very easy to cut yourself.

(1) Start with the teeth facing in. Hold the blade in two places at about the width of your body. Step on the base of the blade to secure it.

(2) Pull your hands together so that the blade crimps outward in a circle.

(3) Cross the blade over itself **(4)** while turning the circle under and **(5)** the blade will fold easily.

Another method requires only one hand. **(6)** Step on the blade and hold it at the top.

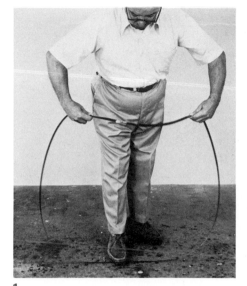

1

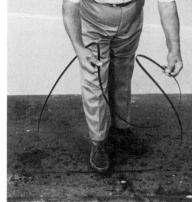

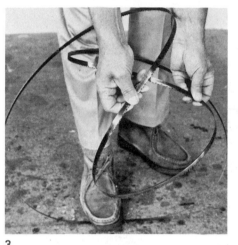

2

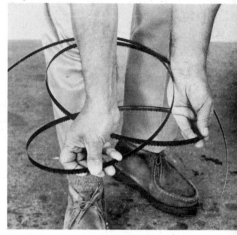

3

4

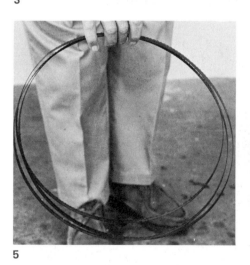

5

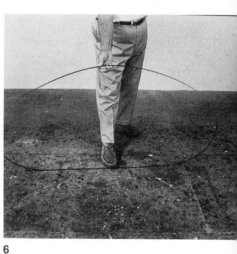

6

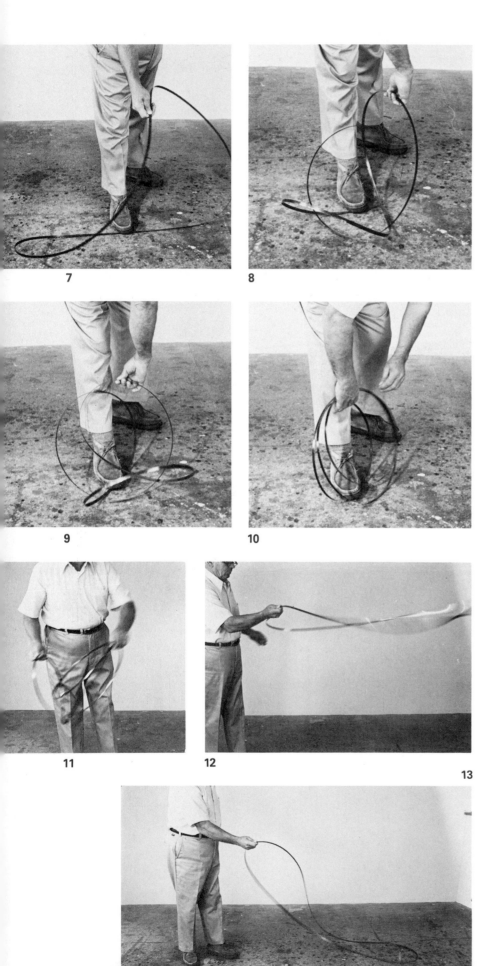

(7) Continue to turn the blade outward, **(8)** around and **(9)** under itself until it folds neatly **(10)**.

To unfold the blade, stand where you have plenty of room **(11)**.

(12) Fling the blade out very firmly away from yourself and **(13)** the blade will spring open. □

7

8

9

10

11

12

13

Preparing Stock
Chapter 4

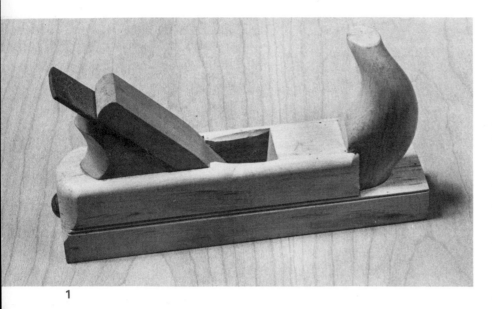

1

2

3

4

5

6

Planes

There are four different lengths of plane used for dressing wood. They are used in sequence to take the wood from rough lumber to clean boards ready to be shaped, glued and so on. Each plane is designed for a different job. But they are all sharpened and set the same way. The four planes are, in order of their use, the scrub plane (or roughing-out plane), the jack plane, the jointer plane and the smoothing plane.

The scrub plane **(1)** is designed to remove large amounts of wood, for example, a high spot if the wood is warped. It can be used going across the grain at an angle, or with the grain. It usually doesn't have a chip-breaker, and the plane iron is ground convex **(2)**. My wooden scrub plane is $9\frac{1}{2}$ in. long, $1\frac{7}{8}$ in. wide, and the blade is $1\frac{1}{4}$ in. wide.

The jack plane **(3)** continues the job of roughing out, but with a little more accuracy than the scrub plane. It is approximately 14 in. long. Its length carries it over the high spots left by the scrub plane, and this ensures a flat surface. A shorter plane would be more apt to travel up and down.

The jointer plane **(4)** is used for jointing and the final flattening out of boards. It is the longest plane — from 22 in. to 24 in. long. The long sole of the plane enables it to flatten out boards efficiently because the sole rides from high spot to high spot until the surface is level. Here again, plane across the grain and at an angle, but finish by planing with the grain.

The smoothing plane **(5)** is the shortest, and is used to begin preparing the surface for finishing. It is about 9 in. to 10 in. long.

When I learned woodworking we used only wooden planes, but now I prefer steel planes. Today all planes are made in either wood or steel, except the scrub plane, which is available only in wood. Steel planes are easier to adjust and they plane well, but they don't slide as easily as wooden planes. More expensive steel planes have corrugated bottoms to make them slide better **(6)**. □

Adjusting Planes

When you buy a new plane, you will have to spend some time to get it to work correctly. Usually the chipbreaker has to be re-fitted so that the shavings will not clog. Put the chipbreaker on the blade and screw it down tight. Hold them up against the light **(1)** and check for light between the chipbreaker and the plane blade. If you can see light between them, remove the chipbreaker and file off the high spots, holding the file at a slight angle **(2)** so that it will take more off in the back of the chipbreaker. This makes for a perfectly tight fit in the front, when the blade and the chipbreaker are together. Keep filing and checking until you no longer see light between the chipbreaker and blade, when they are screwed tight together **(3)**.

Then use a buffer or fine sandpaper to polish the top of the chipbreaker. This surface should be perfectly smooth **(4)** so that the shavings will slide over easily.

The function of the chipbreaker is to prevent the blade from tearing up the surface of the wood. If the chipbreaker is set too far away from the cutting edge of the blade, you might as well use the plane without the chipbreaker. For normal use, the chip breaker should sit back about ⅟₃₂ in. For rough work move it back slightly; for fine work, such as planing curly woods, move it closer to the edge.

The setting of the throat depends on the function of the plane. The throat opening on a smooth plane should be smaller than on a jack plane, and the jointer plane is usually set in between. The setting all depends on the kind of work you are doing.

Wooden planes and iron planes are adjusted differently **(5)**. On a wooden plane **(6)**, the piece of wood in front of the blade on the bottom can be moved back and forth. An iron plane **(7)** is adjusted by moving the whole sophisticated adjusting mechanism, sometimes called the frog.

To adjust the plane iron in the scrub plane (or in any wooden plane) for a deeper cut,

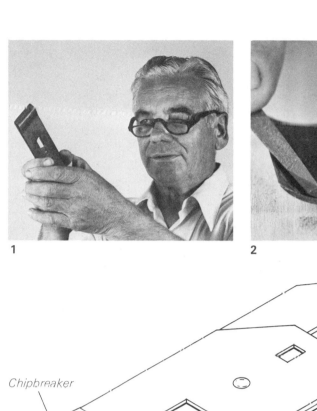

1

2

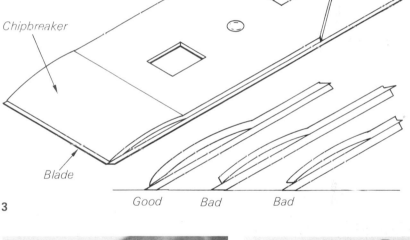

Chipbreaker

Blade

3   Good   Bad   Bad

4

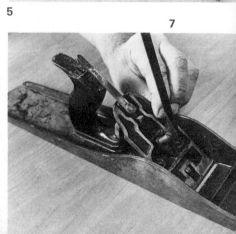

5

6   7

8

9

10

11

12

13

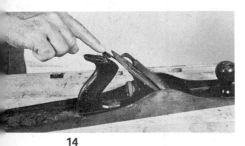

14

15

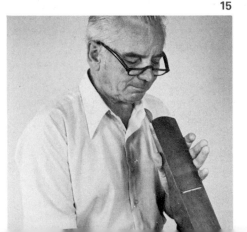

tap the back of the blade **(8)** until enough blade is exposed to give you the depth of the cut you want to make. Notice how the blade is convex, to give a faster cut.

To move the blade back for less of a cut **(9)**, hit the back of the plane with a hammer. Then hit down the wooden wedge to secure the blade. If you want to remove the blade, bang the back of the plane down against the bench and the wedge will loosen, freeing the blade.

Steel planes have more sophisticated adjusting systems. The blade is held in position with a steel wedge **(10)** that is clipped down over a screw **(11)**.

Tension on the blade from the wedge will prevent the blade from coming loose. The screw is tightened **(12)** to create more tension. The screw should be tight but not so tight that you can't push down the clip with your thumb. If the blade loosens, you can tighten the screw again. But once it has been set, it shouldn't need to be adjusted for a long time.

The large screw in the back **(13)** adjusts the depth of the cut. The lower the blade is, the deeper the cut it will take.

The lever in the back **(14)** levels the blade. If you move the lever to the right, the left side of the blade will be raised, and vice versa. The blade must be extended evenly for an even cut.

When you set the blade, check by eye **(15)** that it is parallel with the bottom of the plane, and that it is set to the right depth.

On many planes, especially cheap ones, the sole is not flat. If the sole isn't flat, straighten it out on a belt sander. If a belt sander is not available, glue coarse emery paper on a flat surface and move the plane back and forth until it is flat. The latter is a painstaking job. When I'm first truing up a plane sole on a belt sander, I make the sole of the jointer plane a fraction of an inch convex ($\frac{1}{64}$ in. or less) from front to back, so that when I join boards together they will have edges slightly concave along their length. This is what I want for a good glue joint (see p. 54). ☐

Sharpening Planes and Chisels

A plane blade must be sharp to perform correctly. Sharpening requires practice and must be learned. The same techniques used to sharpen plane blades are also used to sharpen chisels.

The blade must be sharpened perfectly straight across the cutting edge. Don't make the edge concave or the corners will dig into the wood. In fact, when I sharpen a blade for rough cutting I usually make the blade just slightly convex so the corners won't dig in.

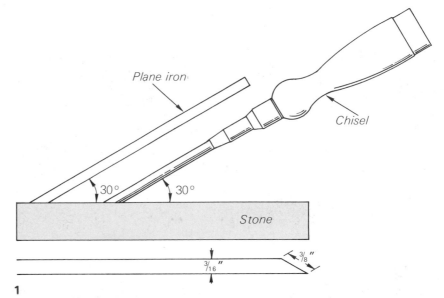

(1) For both plane blades and chisel blades, the cutting edge should be beveled at approximately 30°, which makes the bevel twice as long as the blade is thick. For example, if the blade is ³⁄₁₆ in thick, the bevel should be about ³⁄₈ in. long. The initial sharpening can be done **(2)** on a power sander, **(3)** a portable belt sander mounted upside-down in the bench vise, or **(4)** on a stone. I usually use a power sander because it works considerably faster. If you use a sander, be sure to keep moving the blade without changing the angle. Don't use belts coarser than 120 grit, or bad pits will develop that you'll never get out. Old belts are fine. Don't let the blade get too hot or you will ruin the temper and destroy the blade. Either stop to allow the blade to cool, or dip the blade in water before continuing.

If I use stones, I prefer a wet/dry carborundum medium and coarse combination stone, which I use without water. If the blade isn't nicked or too uneven I start with the medium side. If the blade is in rough shape, I start with the coarse side and then go to the medium side. Again, use the entire surface. Make sure the stone is not hollowed. If it is, the blade will not have the correct bevel angle.

In any case, sharpen the blade until any nicks or uneven areas in the bevel are removed. The first step is completed when there is an even burr across the back of the blade. The blade is then ready for honing.

(5,6) I generally use a buffer with a polishing compound for steel. I made this buffer for my own use only. For anyone

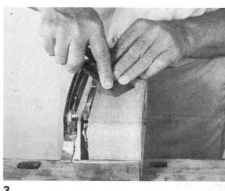

7

8

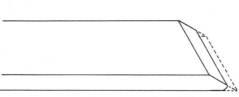

*Blade back becomes beveled
if ground on hollowed stone*

9

else, guards should be put on, in which case it would be cheaper to buy a commercial buffer or grinder already equipped with guards.

If I use a stone for honing I prefer a Belgian clay stone with water, not oil. I don't like oilstones because the oil gets on your hands, the bench and many times on the work, too. Keep your fingers in the same position on the blade so that the blade doesn't rock. Stone or buff the bevel side first **(7)**, and then **(8)** stone any burr off the back; keeping the blade perfectly flat against the stone. Continue to buff the bevel side and the back of the blade until the burr is gone and the blade is sharp. In the honing stage, it is especially important that the stone is not hollowed, or the flat side of the blade would get a bevel on the back **(9)**. Either hold the stone in your hand, keeping the angle constant, or mount the stone in the bench vise.

(10) A sharp plane blade should cut clean, crisp shavings.

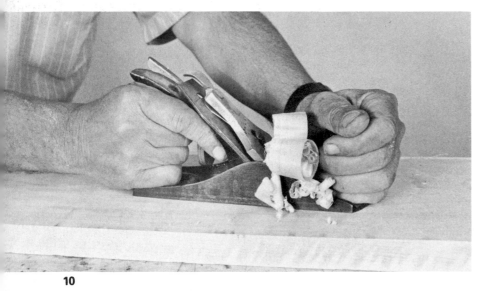

10

Preparing Boards by Hand

To prepare a board using hand tools, first **(1)** cut it to rough length and width. Then check with a straightedge **(2)** to see if the board is straight. It may be either concave, convex or twisted. Use a scrub plane **(3)** to remove the high parts.

I always use the scrub plane first at an angle to the grain **(4)**, and then diagonally across in the other direction. The grain won't tear out as easily as if the plane were used with the grain. Continue with the scrub plane until the board is just about flat. Use a straight board **(5)** to check flatness. With the jack plane **(6)**, remove the planer marks left by the scrub plane. Use the same diagonal pattern as before, until you are nearly finished. I finish off the board by planing with the grain.

1

2

3

4

5

6

7

8

9

10

To check if the board is twisted, take two pieces of straight wood the same width. Place one at each end of the board **(7)**. **(8)** Sight along the sticks to see if the two pieces are parallel. If not, correct by continuing to plane off the high points.

When the piece is finally flat, smooth the board **(9)** with the jointer plane. Pushing down in the front of the plane when starting at the beginning of the board and pushing down at the back of the plane at the end of the board will prevent rounding the edges.

The board is now flat on one side only. If you had been using power tools, the jointer would have gotten you to this stage. Now you are ready to get the other side flat, parallel to the first side and the right thickness. With power tools, you would use a thickness planer to accomplish this, but with hand tools you must use a marking gauge and hand planes. **(10)** Scribe the thickness you want on all the edges of the board. Then go through the same planing procedure as before, using the planes in the same order. I don't square the edges after the first face is leveled because the edges could be torn while thickness-planing with the scrub plane. □

The Marking Gauge

On a new marking gauge **(1)**, the steel pin that scribes the line into the wood is rounded down to a point. When scribing across the grain, the rounded point scratches the fibers and makes a fuzzy line. Therefore the pin of every new marking gauge must be refiled.

First, file half the thickness of the pin flat **(2)**, at right angles to the wooden surface of the tool.

Then bevel the other side of the pin toward the inside **(3)**.

If you are right-handed, the edge that will face you when you pull the tool should be filed as sharp as a knife **(4)**. If you are left-handed, you can reverse the filing to make the gauge easier for you to use.

With the bevel filed in toward the movable guide piece, the guide will be pushed up against the edge of the board to be scribed.

The difference that refiling makes is easy to see **(5)**. The round point makes a fuzzy line (top), while the refiled point makes a crisp, clear line (bottom) with no tendency to wander with the grain. □

1

2

3

4

5

1

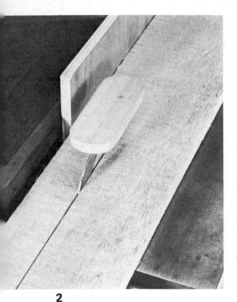

2

3

Rough-Ripping

To get maximum thickness out of a board, I always rip it to approximate width when it is rough lumber. This way, if one side of the board is slightly thinner or is twisted or warped, you won't have to plane the whole board to the thickness of the thinnest section. Remember to allow for jointing the edges and subsequently ripping the board to exact size when you make the first rip cut. A safe estimate is to add about ⅜ in. or more to the width of the board. Be sure the edge that will ride against the fence is straight, or your measurement will be thrown off.

When rough-ripping boards on the circular saw, I always screw a short piece of wood to the front of the fence **(1)**. This piece, which should stop at the center of the blade, is necessary because a board tends to open or close up at the saw kerf as it is ripped. Without the half-length fence **(2)**, a board that is opening up would be forced into the blade. This creates heat and gums up the blade. If forced through, the board may bind or the blade might be ruined permanently.

If a board is twisted so much that planing it would leave you with a very thin piece, rip the board in half, joint each half, then glue the pieces back together. This way you can use more of the thickness of the board.

For ripping the edges on rough boards, I use a jig **(3,4)** that helps me cut a straight edge on a piece of lumber with rough edges or an irregular shape. First fit a strip of wood into the groove of the table saw flush with the top of the groove. Then screw and glue that onto a piece of either solid wood or plywood that is approximately 8 in. wide by 8 ft. long. I locate the piece so that one edge is close to, but doesn't touch, the side of the sawblade.

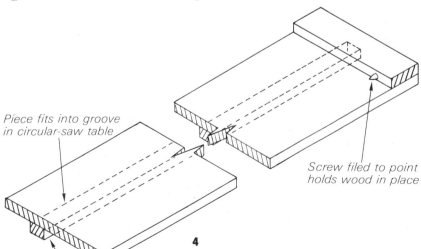

Piece fits into groove
in circular-saw table

Screw filed to point
holds wood in place

4

Slightly less than distance from sawblade to groove

Next make a piece of wood several inches wide and as long as the width of the jig, in this case, 8 in., and insert a screw into the piece. Saw off the head of the screw with the end sticking out slightly. After filing the end to a sharp point, screw and glue this piece across the front edge of the jig **(5)**. The screw end combined with the fence it sits in will secure one end of the piece to be sawn. **(6)** Some sheets of #50 or coarser sandpaper glued to the top surface of the jig will prevent the piece from sliding.

Lay the wood on top of the jig and push one end firmly into the point of the screw **(7)**. This holds the piece in place. Press the wood down into the sandpaper and cut one edge **(8)**. Slide the jig through the blade **(9)** with the holding block in front.

Once the wood has one straight edge cut, use that edge against the fence and rip a parallel cut on the other edge.   . ☐

5

6

7

8

9

1

2

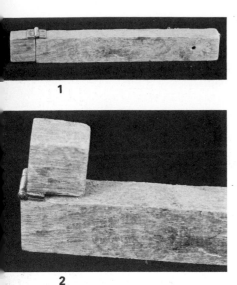

3

4

Jig for Cutting Wood to Length

When I have a quantity of wood to square and cut to the same length, I have found this jig **(1)** to be a great timesaver. It is simply a piece of scrap wood with 1 in. cut off one end. **(2)** The cut-off piece is fastened back again with a loose hinge. Slice off ⅛ in. from the underside of the 1-in. piece so that it opens and closes more easily. I clamp the jig to a board attached to my miter gauge. **(3)** To use, lift the hinged end up, square one end of the board (I'm using scrap here) flip the piece end for end, so the same edge is against the miter gauge **(4)**. Drop the hinged piece and cut the other end of the wood to length **(5)**. This is a very inexpensive way to have a well-functioning stopping mechanism. There are some much fancier, more complicated and expensive devices on the market, but I have been using this one satisfactorily for close to 50 years. □

5

Jig for Sawing Square Cutoffs

This jig replaces the miter gauge for square crosscutting on the table saw. It is much easier to use than the miter gauge when working with large pieces. The jig is simple to make and should last a long time.

(1) Cut two hardwood strips to fit into the grooves in the saw table. The strips should fit well but slide easily.

Place the slides in the grooves and **(2)** glue and **(3)** screw a piece of plywood to them. I used ½-in. veneer-core plywood. Don't use a rough piece—the surfaces should be relatively smooth.

Whenever you insert a screw into a hard piece of wood, it is advisable to coat the screw threads lightly with **(4)** paraffin or soap to help the screw go in easier and prevent it from breaking. This is especially true with big screws, which are usually harder to screw in.

Once the plywood is fastened to the slides, raise the sawblade to make a kerf in the plywood **(5)**. I prefer to stop the sawcut before the back, which makes the piece more stable. If you run the cut all the way through you will have to put a heavy piece of solid wood in the back as well as in the front

(6) Glue and screw on the front piece, made of hardwood about 2 in. thick. **(7)** Be sure that the piece is square to the sawcut and square to the plywood table. This "fence" has to be higher in the center than the height of the blade when it is fully raised. (I make it about 3 in. higher than the full height of the blade.) To lighten the jig, I leave the full height only in the center section.

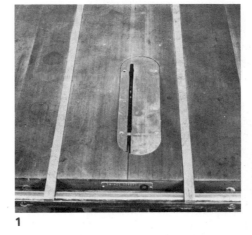

1

2

3

4

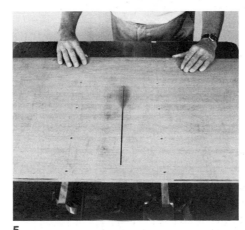

5

6

7

8

Before the glue sets, make a test cut **(8)** to check the squareness of the jig. If the jig is out of square in either direction you can still correct it. **(9)** I was lucky the first time, and was very proud.

The jig can be used for many years. **(10)** Rub the slides and the bottom with paraffin to help the jig slide more easily.   □

9

10

The Jointer

After the circular table saw, I feel that the jointer and the thickness planer are the most important big machines in a woodshop, especially for a person who wants to make a living from woodworking. These two machines are a big investment but will pay for themselves over the years. An old out dated jointer and thickness planer can sometimes be bought quite inexpensively and will usually do as good a job as a new machine. Don't buy an old jointer with a square head—it's too dangerous. The smallest jointer I would buy would be a 6-in. model, (an 8-in. one is preferable) with a 1-hp motor. The smallest thickness planer I'd buy is a 12-in. one with a 2-hp motor.

Jointing by machine   A jointer is a machine that planes, joints or surfaces a board, ending up with one side perfectly flat **(1)**. The table in the front of the rotating knives is called the infeed table, and the one in the back is the outfeed table. The difference in height between the infeed and outfeed is the thickness of wood planed off with each pass. When setting the knives, be sure they are level or parallel with the top of the outfeed table.

On a jointer with a round cutterhead, I would never run a piece shorter than 10 in. Jointers with square cutterheads have a larger opening. These aren't made anymore, but if you buy a used one it might be of this type. I would never run anything shorter than 15 in. on such a jointer. Never run end grain over the jointer—it is too dangerous. End grain is very hard and often shatters rather than cutting. Don't pass the edges of plywood over a jointer either—the glue will put nicks in the blade.

Setting jointer knives   Knives on a jointer should be parallel to the outfeed table and all at the same height. Use a straight stick to set the jointer knives. *First, unplug the machine.* Then make a pencil mark on the stick at the beginning of the outfeed table **(2)**, while the cutterhead is below the table.

(3) Then move the cutterhead forward (carrying the stick with it) and **(4)** make a second mark, again at the beginning of the outfeed table **(5)**.

Now move the stick to the opposite end of the knife and repeat the procedure. If the stick moves the same amount, the knife is parallel to the outfeed table. If it does not, loosen the nuts that hold the knife in place and correct before retightening. When that knife is parallel, be sure to tighten all the nuts. Move to the next knife and set it in the same way, using the same stick and the same two markings (so the height of the second blade is the same as the first). Continue until all the knives are aligned. Be sure all the knives are secured before you start the machine. Raise the outfeed table so it is level with the knives.

Sharpening the knives   An easy way to sharpen the knives without removing them is to use a router. Remove the plastic plate from the base of the router and **(6)** screw on a piece of ¾-in. plywood. Place a medium-grit grindstone in the router. The two grooves in the bottom of the plywood have nothing to do with the sharpening process—I used a scrap piece of plywood.

1

2

3

4

5

6

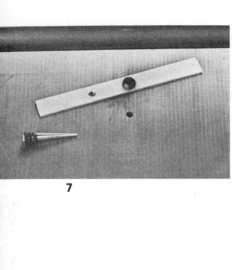

7

8

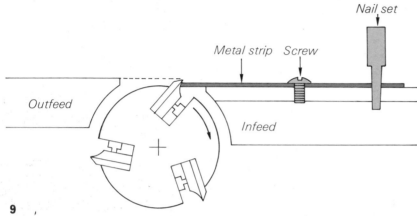

Nail set

Metal strip   Screw

Outfeed

Infeed

9

You must be able to control the position of the knives so they will all be ground the same amount. To do this, drill two holes in the center of the infeed table **(7)**. The first hole, closer to the knives, is about 1½ in. from the opening for the cutterhead. The second hole is directly behind the first, about 3 in. from the edge of the opening. Thread the first hole to receive a ³⁄₁₆-in. or ¼-in. screw. Then cut a thin but stiff piece of sheet aluminum or steel about 7 in. long. Drill a hole in the center of the metal strip about 2½ in. from the end of the piece on the side closer to the cutterhead. Be sure the screw fits snugly into the hole. Then drill a second hole in the strip corresponding to the second hole in the table. The exact measurements may vary with different jointers. The important thing is that the metal strip keep all the knives in the same position.

Fasten the metal strip to the table and **(8)** insert a steel pin into the second hole (I used the end of a nail set). Push the cutterhead tight up against the metal strip. Lower the infeed table until the bevel of the knives is parallel with the outfeed table **(9)**. Secure the cutterhead by inserting wooden wedges at both outside ends of the knife head.

Set the router on the outfeed table with the piece of plywood resting on the table. Set the depth of the grindstone so that it just touches the bevel of the blade. Be sure you are wearing proper face and eye protection. Start the router and **(10)** carefully move it back and forth over the blade until the stone stops cutting. Be sure to keep the plywood piece flat on the table.

When the first knife is ground, remove the wooden wedges and the tapered steel pin. Swing the metal strip out of the way and move the cutterhead so that the next knife is on top. Reposition the metal strip, insert the steel pin and wedge the cutterhead again. Continue sharpening until all the knives are ground. Do not change the height of either the infeed or outfeed tables, or of the grindstone in the router.

The knives are sharp when a small burr appears on the back of each knife along its whole length. It is not necessary to remove this burr. If you want to make the knives a little sharper, you can hone each one by

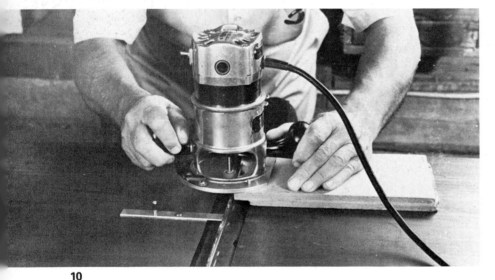

10

11   With the grain →   ← Against the grain

hand with a honing stone. I usually don't bother.

If the knives still are not sharp after one grinding, repeat the process. They can be sharpened this way about five times before you will have to reposition them farther out. After each sharpening you have to raise the outfeed table to the same height as the knives.

Operating the jointer   The infeed table controls how much of a cut is to be taken off the boards. In a soft wood, I would never take off more than $\frac{1}{16}$ in. in one pass. In extremely hard wood or a wood with unusual grain pattern (like curly maple), I would take much less at each pass.

Before you pass wood over the jointer, look at the edge of the board to see which way the grain runs. Running the board so that the cutting action goes with the grain produces the smoothest edge **(11)**. However, the grain sometimes reverses direction in the middle of the piece and you cannot avoid roughing up some of the wood. Either handplane the board or take the roughness out later by scraping and sanding after milling is complete.

When using the jointer for a board that is slightly bowed, either take the same amount off of each end first or start jointing in the middle to correct the bowing on one face. Here **(12)** I took it off each end. When one face is roughly straightened out, feed the wood in again with the straight face down. When approximately five to six inches have passed over the knives, push the wood down on the outfeed table and ease up the pressure over the infeed table **(13)**. Because the board is perfectly flat when passing over the knives, putting pressure only on the outfeed table keeps the board flat and straight. Otherwise, if the board is twisted and all the pressure is only on the infeed table, the board will continue to be twisted and the twist will get jointed into the piece so that very shortly you will have a piece of uneven thickness that follows the twist.

Once one face is flat, joint the edge. First put a square at the end of the infeed table **(14)** and check that the fence is square. Then **(15)** joint the edge, keeping the face of the board tight against the fence. When

matching edges are jointed, check to see how they fit. If they do not fit tightly for their entire length, joint the boards again. Note: The safeguard has been removed for clarity of the photograph.

(16) Here you can see the joint is convex. The boards have to be jointed again. To correct a convex edge, flatten the curve by running the center of the board over the jointer. Then take one full pass. Whenever you joint an edge for a glue joint, pass the board over the jointer slowly so that the surface gets very smooth. If this burnishes the surface, the knives need resharpening.

When you are jointing boards to be edge-glued, joint each board with the opposite face against the fence. If the fence is slightly off square, the next board will be off square the opposite way and the two will fit together, gluing up straight. But the two faces of the board must be parallel, to use this technique. That is, the board should have been put through a thickness planer.

To demonstrate this point, the fence was set well off square. **(17)** Note how the edge of the board slopes down under the square. Even if the two edges are not square, but the opposite faces of the board are run against the fence, the two boards will still glue up straight **(18)**.   ☐

12

13

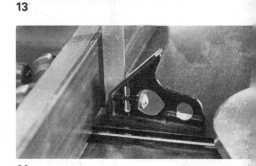

14

15

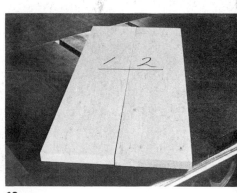

16

17

18

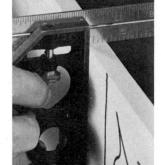

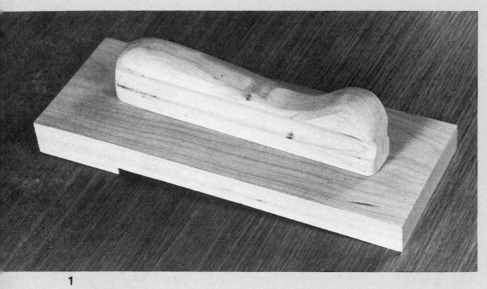

1

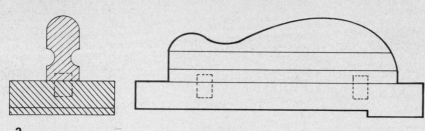

2

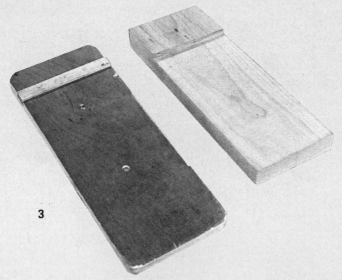

3

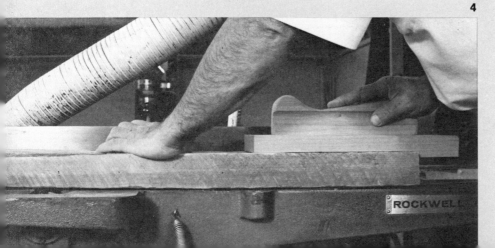

4

Push-Stick

Always use a push-stick when running wood over the jointer. It is much safer, since your hands are sitting on the push-stick and not on the wood, where they could possibly slip off into the knives.

(1) I use a push-stick with a handle long enough that I can keep both hands on it when I run short pieces over the jointer. The sides of the handle are grooved so that my hands fit comfortably and joined to the base with dowels **(2)**.

(3) The push-stick on the right is made out of one piece of wood, so there is end grain pushing against the back of the board when you use it. The push-stick on the left is a piece of plywood with another piece of wood screwed and glued to the bottom of the back. I feel this type of push-stick is too dangerous. The edge that backs up the board is long grain, which will eventually get banged up and start to break.

(4) Even with a long board, always use a push-stick on the end so your hands or fingers won't slip into the knives. ☐

Resawing by Hand

Resawing is a way of getting thinner boards out of thicker boards or of producing beautiful bookmatched wood (panels with mirror-image grain patterns).

When you resaw a board by hand, begin by marking the cutting line on both sides and on the end. Clamp the board in the bench vise at an angle and **(1)** start sawing from the back corner of the end down the side. The sawcut will be at an angle.

(2) Follow the line on both surfaces. Once you have a cut that reaches partway from the back corner down one side, turn the board around in the vise. The angle cut will then be in the back.

With the board clamped straight in the vise, insert the saw in the cut in the back **(3)** and start sawing following the top line to the front. The first sawcut will guide the saw, and the board will be started with a very even cut.

(4) A correctly set saw will follow the lines easily in both the front and back.   □

1

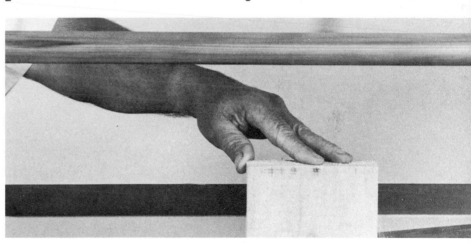

2

3

4

1

2

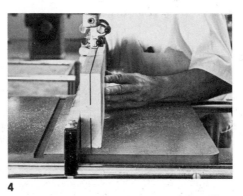

3

4

5

Resawing on the Table Saw

It is considerably easier and faster to resaw a board by machine. A band saw is fastest (see p. 28). If the board is not too wide, it can be resawn on the circular saw **(1)**. Set the fence to the right width, and **(2)** cut from both edges. The board has to be square and milled cleanly for the process to work accurately. Don't take more than one inch with each pass or the sawblade will heat up. Continue flipping the board. If the board is too wide to finish off on the table saw, finish the cutting of the center section on the band saw **(3,4)** or with a handsaw.

Start with a board as thick as possible, because wood usually warps after it has been resawn. **(5)** After this board was resawn, it opened up from the center lengthwise. If the board was not thick enough, there would not be enough left to thickness-plane and straighten out the board.

(6) The boards will have to be jointed and thickness planed or hand planed to make the faces clean.

(7) Here are the resawn pieces, planed clean. Note the bookmatched, mirror-image grain pattern. **(8)** If the wood is dried evenly **(a)**, the resawn pieces will look like this. If the wood is drier on the outside than on the inside **(b)**, the two resawn pieces will curve toward the outside. If the board is drier on the inside **(c)**, the board will curve toward the inside.

Remember that if a board has to be resawn, there is a 75% chance that it will warp after it is cut. You must allow for that. It is a good idea to resaw the boards a few days before jointing and thickness-planing them. This way you allow the wood to stablilize a little more before you mill them to final size.

The same thing usually happens when you joint and thickness-plane a board and more is taken off one side than the other. For example, if a board is 1½ in. thick and the wood has to be planed down to 1 in., if the full ½-in. excess is removed from one side there is a great chance the board will warp **(d)**. The same thing is true if you turn or rout out a large mass of wood on only one side of something such as you might for a tabletop or a tray.   ☐

6

7

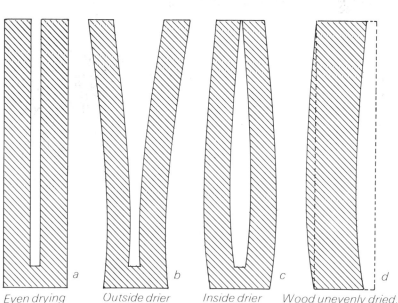

Even drying   *Outside drier than inside*   *Inside drier than outside*   *Wood unevenly dried, then most of the wood is removed from one side as might be done with the thickness planer, router or lathe. This piece might move one way or the other, and usually does after a day or two.*

Movement of resawn wood

8

1

3

The Thickness Planer

A thickness planer **(1)** makes the top surface of a board parallel to the surface that runs against the bed of the machine, so it is used to make boards an even thickness. Usually, one surface of the board has already been made flat with a jointer or hand planes before putting it through the thicknesser. The cutterhead is usually above the table and the knives have to be set parallel to the table surface below. The table can be moved up and down in fine increments to provide varying thicknesses. There are also two rollers in the table that can be moved up and down independently from the table **(2)**.

There are two spring-loaded rollers above the table, one located in front of the cutterhead and one behind it. These simultaneously press the board down against the table and feed the board through the machine. The front roller is corrugated and does the most pushing. Often this roller will leave marks in the wood, which the cutterhead usually planes out. The back roller is smooth, so that the wood isn't marked up after it is planed.

A handle controls the power feed, so that the wood can be fed forward, stopped or pushed backwards. These directions are usually marked forward, neutral and reverse. The location of the power feed varies among different makes. Always place yourself so that you can reach the handles easily. If something goes wrong, you have to be able to stop or reverse the feed immediately. Never bend down in front of the thickness planer to look between the table and the cutterhead while the machine is running. The cutting action is toward the front, so if a piece should break off, it will fly back right at you. Always stay to the side of the machine. If it is necessary to glance into the machine, at least position yourself to the side.

If there are 12 in. between the two power-feed rollers, never run a board through that is less than 15 in. long or the piece will be completely chewed up. The minimum length of board will vary with the size of the machine. Remember to account for the board catching at the front roller, traveling the distance between the rollers, and then catching again at the back roller. Check the manufacturer's instructions for your machine.

Don't always run the wood through the center of the planer. Use the whole bed so the blades wear evenly. If you have to remove a lot of wood from a board, take half off each side, so the board won't warp.

Plane with the grain. **(3)** Here the wood is being passed through the thickness planer. **(4)** The upper corrugated roller is clearly seen. You can see that the wood is sitting off from the table in the corner. The rollers will push down the wood so that the top surface won't be planed off more where the wood is sitting higher off the table.

(5) The wood emerges from the machine with the top surface planed clean and parallel to the bottom surface.

If you want to plane a piece that is ¼ in. or less in thickness, always clamp a board to the table **(6)**. The board must run all the way through the machine and be clamped at both ends. (The board is clamped to the table because the two rollers in the table bottom stick up a fraction of an inch above the surface. Thin wood would begin to vibrate over these rollers as it was passed through, and the piece would be chewed up.) Position the clamps so that they don't interfere with the travel of the board, and keep the board wide enough so that if the piece feeds in at an angle or somehow gets cocked, it will not slide off the board.   □

4

5

6

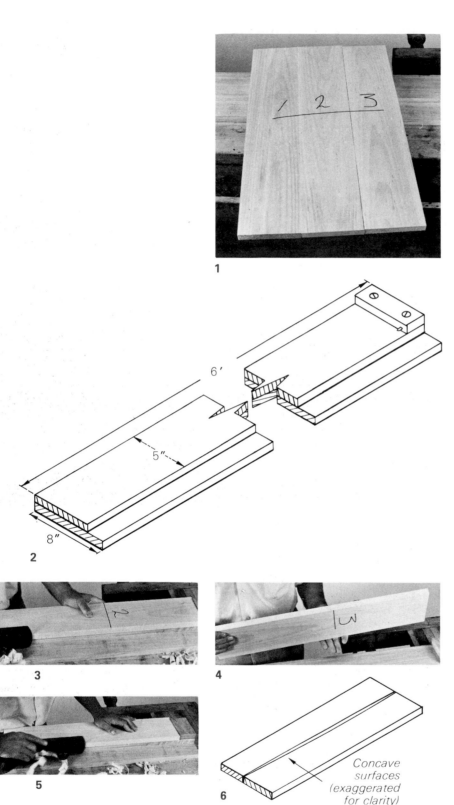

1

2

3

4

5

6

Concave surfaces (exaggerated for clarity)

6'

5"

8"

Edge-Joining Boards

When the boards are thickness-planed, rip them (if necessary) to the desired width. Then match them and **(1)** mark the top side with numbers so you know how they should go together when you glue them up. You can joint them on a jointer, or, even better, by hand. Hand planes leave a perfectly smooth glue surface.

Use hardwood when making the jig **(2)** for jointing boards together. Maple or cherry or any other hardwood will be strong, and the plane will slide more easily against the wood. It is a good idea to put paraffin or wax where the plane slides. When you use the jointing jig, put the first board with its number up and the matching edge on board two with the number two down. **(3)** Then joint the other edge of number two board with its number up and finally **(4,5)** number three down. This ensures that even if the plane or its blade is not square, the boards will still join together perfectly for gluing.

The right way to glue boards long grain to long grain is without using dowels. Run the edges over the jointer slowly, or even better, use a hand jointer plane, and get a slightly concave surface. Then glue the boards together. This puts a slight pressure on the ends. When the wood dries and gives off moisture at the ends first, the pressure is released and the ends will not split **(6)**. At the same time, fewer clamps are used.

If the wood is glued together using this method and we try to break it apart, generally it will break somewhere other than at the joints. If it did break at the joints, it would take wood from both pieces, which proves we have a joint as strong as the material itself. There is no reason for putting a spline or tongue and groove in the joint to get more glue surface. Furniture factories like to use tongue-and-groove joinery because it allows machines to line up boards. But for individual craftsmen, it's a waste of time.

To check if the joint is correct before gluing, put the two boards together **(7)** so that when twisting one board back and forth the other one follows. If this doesn't happen, the board is convex, not concave.

(8) Put glue on both edges. I usually use Titebond glue and put it on with a squeeze bottle. I then use the cheapest brush I can find — my finger. Spread the glue thinly but evenly.

(9) Put the clamp in the center first and get all the boards flush in the center.

(10) Use a block and hammer the boards down until the joints meet flush.

If you can't get the joints flush, stop hammering. **(11)** Put paper and blocks on both sides of the board over the joint and put on another clamp. Tighten the clamp until the joint is flush. Then remove the blocks. The paper prevents the block from being glued to the board.

Now put two more clamps on **(12)**. I put them on the underside so that if the pressure of the clamps bows the wood, the alternated clamps will counteract each other. When gluing wood together, just squeeze the clamp tight enough with your hand. You should see a slight squeeze-out of glue along both sides of a properly glued joint. Don't use wrenches, pipes or the like to force the joint tight. If forcing is necessary, there is definitely something wrong. One other thing most books advise (but I hardly ever do) is to clamp a 2x4 across the boards to keep them straight. This shouldn't be necessary if clamps are alternated on each side and the wood is planed correctly.

7

8

9

10

11

12

13

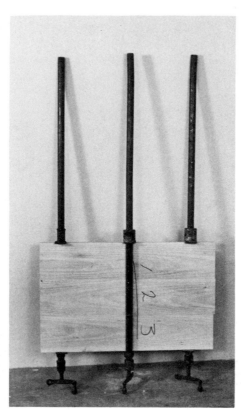

14

15

Using a stick and paper **(13)**, clean the glue off both sides while the glue is still wet. Try not to let the clamp touch the glue. If it does, the clamp might stain the wood black because of the tannic acid in the wood.

The line of the joint should not be visible. If it is, the joint is not going to hold. Any gap between the pieces will be filled with glue, and glue is not strong on its own. If you pour glue out and make a sheet of it, you can see that the glue breaks easily. But if you have a good glue joint and you try and split the joint along the glue line the piece will split, taking wood from both pieces being joined.

When you set the boards aside to dry, make sure that just one corner isn't resting against the wall. The weight of the clamps will twist the unsupported wood. **(14)** Be sure both clamps rest against the wall.

When the glue is dry, plane the board level again. Start out using the plane at an angle **(15)**, but this time use only the jointer plane. After one side is done, mark the thickness around the edges with a marking gauge and plane the other side, being careful to follow the thickness lines. You now have one wide board.

If the piece is glued together right, the wood has not warped and the thickness is not critical, just plane and sand the board.   ☐

Clamps

There are many different clamps available, some designed for specific jobs. But for regular clamping, I prefer quick-action clamps **(1)**. They work fast, are very flexible and do an excellent job. In my shop, the smallest clamp is 2 in. deep, with an opening capacity of 6½ in. I have several clamps 4 in. deep (opening capacity is 8½, 12½, 18½ and 32½ in.). I also have a few 7-in. deep clamps with an opening capacity of 18½ in., which I use when the clamp has to reach in deeper.

If you are buying your first clamps, I'd advise getting some 2 in. deep with an opening capacity of 6½ in. Then buy some 4 in. deep, opening capacity 18 in. The difference between, for example, a 12-in. and an 18-in. clamp, is only a few dollars, but the wider clamp can do more work. Later you can add different sizes—it is easier to work with the right-sized clamp for the job.

For bar clamps, I use pipe clamps. They are less expensive, and the same fixtures can be used with ¾-in. black pipes of various lengths.   □

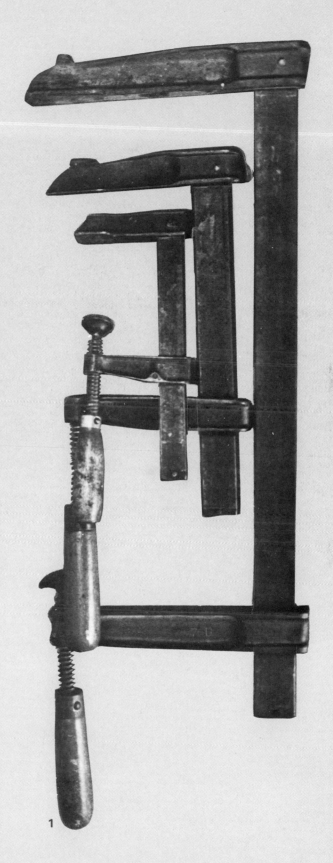

1

1

Straightening Warped Wood

If a board warps before the joint is cut, and the joints are cut while the board is still warped, the joints will never fit correctly. **(1)** In this picture, the convex side is up to show how warped the board is. To straighten out the board so the joints can be cut, wet a cloth and place it on the concave side of the board.

Using a hot iron **(2)**, steam the board until it is straight. **(3)** The board will straighten out very fast. Then hurry up and cut your joints while the board is straight. Even if the board warps again, the pieces will go back together straight because the joints were cut when the boards were straight.   ☐

2

3

Dovetails
Chapter 5

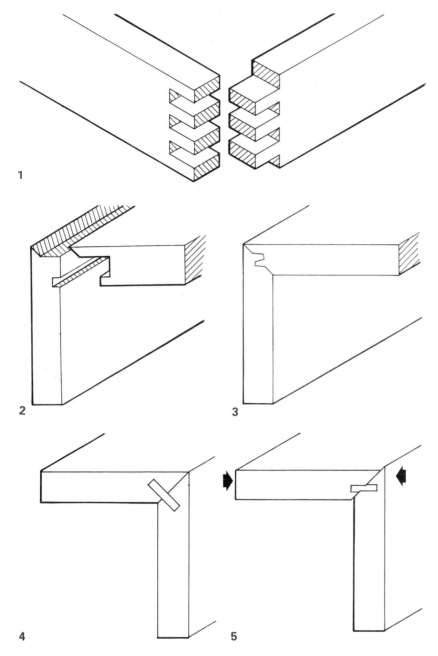

1

2

3

4

5

Carcase Joinery

Furniture construction is broken down into two main categories: frame and carcase. In frame construction, relatively narrow boards are joined — usually with a mortise and tenon joint — as in a chair or table base, or in a frame and panel door. In carcase construction, boards are joined end to end using dovetails, tongue-and-groove and the like, as in a drawer or hutch. When designing a carcase, as in a box, drawer, bureau or the like, a beginner may find it difficult to know which joint to choose. Some joints are excellent in plywood but weak in solid wood, and vice-versa. Many beginners are so concerned with the "craft" aspect that they design in the most complicated techniques. They use a complex joint where a joint easier to make would work just as well. I always choose the strongest but easiest joint to construct. I cannot see spending time over-constructing a piece. And I expect my furniture to last long after I do.

Except as noted, most carcase joints described in this book are strong enough for all carcase applications. So the choice is really yours — more a question of esthetics and construction time than of utility.

Most joints can be made by hand, but they are usually more easily and precisely made by machine. A table saw is the most widely used and best-suited machine for making joints.

Dovetailing is one of the strongest and most attractive methods of joining the ends of boards together. This is true if you are going to make joints by hand. But most carcase joints lend themselves to machine fabrication. The closest machine joint to a dovetail is a finger or box joint **(1)**. Because of the greater number of pins and the resulting total glue surface, it is stronger than a dovetail, far easier to make and just as attractive.

The lock miter **(2)** is used for either solid wood or plywood. Its advantages are that it is hidden to the outside, and that it requires clamping in only one direction, because of the built-in locking action.

The double-tongued lock miter **(3)** is the best and fastest production joint for plywood but it requires a shaper with special knives. Only one shaper setting is required — the first piece is run through vertically, the second horizontally. The same clamping benefit holds true here. I use this joint only in plywood. In production work, the time saved pays for the relatively high cost of the cutter.

The spline miter **(4)** really lends itself to plywood, but can be used in solid wood on smaller pieces such as boxes. The grain direction of the spline must follow that of the pieces being joined. The spline should be placed $\frac{1}{5}$ to $\frac{1}{6}$ of the way in from the inside corner so as not to weaken the corner. Because of the 45° angle, all pieces must be glued up simultaneously, a real disadvantage in a piece with many parts. Also, a lot of clamps (in all directions) are required to ensure tight glue lines.

A lesser-used spline miter with a parallel spline **(5)** has several advantages but can be used only in plywood. This spline is not as strong as the diagonal one. The spline slots are minutely offset (about $\frac{1}{32}$ in.). Clamps are needed only parallel to the spline, and the offset pulls the pieces tightly together. The ease of clamping this joint is a real advantage. You can glue the inside members and sides first, and when they dry, glue on the top and bottom.

(6) A corner tongue and groove, rounded or square, is good for either plywood or solid wood. In plywood the grain of the corner piece must run lengthwise along the edging. However, in solid woods, the grain must run in the same direction as the grain of the sides so that expansion is constant. The grain should run diagonally from tongue to tongue. Any shaped corner molding can be used. The inside is shaped first, the pieces are glued together, and then the outside is shaped.

The doweled miter **(7)** is used where structure is not crucial — in small boxes, knick-knack cabinets, spice racks, etc. It is easy to make and aligns itself correctly for gluing because of the dowels. A dowel center or a brad is useful for transferring the position of one hole to its corresponding hole. This joint works in solid wood or plywood.

I generally do not use a butt joint with dowels **(8)** but when I do, I find it advan-

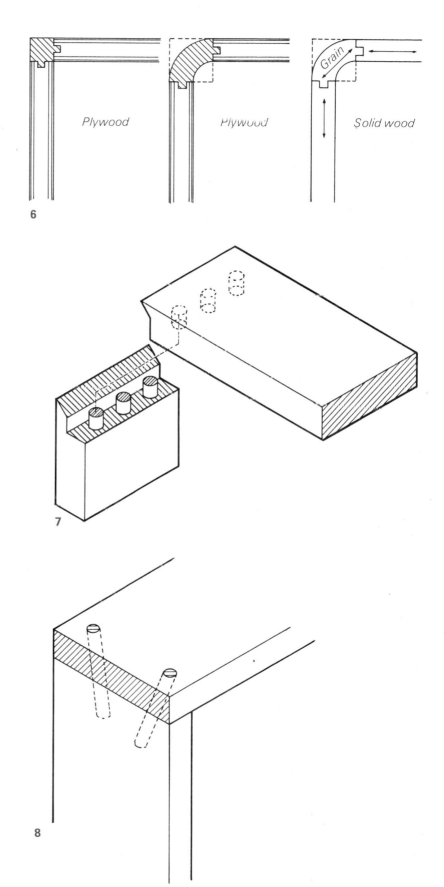

Plywood

Plywood

Solid wood

Grain

6

7

8

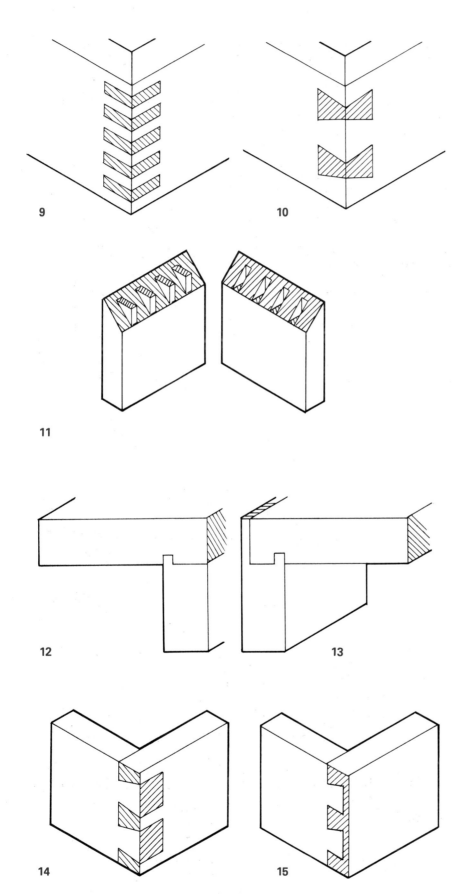

9

10

11

12

13

14

15

tageous to angle the dowels. This adds needed strength to the joint.

Several joints are made by cutting a miter, gluing the corners together, and then cutting slots to receive splines. These joints have great strength and pleasing decorative qualities. With jigs, they can be made extremely quickly. The mock finger joint **(9)** resembles a finger joint without the alternating fingers.

A mock dovetail **(10)** is made similarly, but using a router mounted in a table. If desired, a contrasting wood can be used for splines as a decorative detail.

For hidden splines **(11)**, the slots can be cut using a router with a machine (or your own) dovetail jig. This joint is considerably stronger than a full-blind dovetail because of the greater glue surface.

The tongue and rabbet **(12)** is not the strongest joint but is good enough for the back of a drawer (although not as strong as a dovetail). It is very easy to make. The proportions must be strictly adhered to, as they are determined by factors of strength. The groove should be no deeper than ¼ to ⅕ of the board's thickness, and the same goes for the thickness of the tongue.

The half-blind tongue and rabbet **(13)** is like a lock miter without the miter. It is particularly good for drawer fronts, but in that case be sure to put the drawer stop somewhere other than in the front because of the joint's limited strength. This joint can also be made with a router.

Machine-cut dovetails made with a router and dovetail jig are useful where great quantities must be cut, or where the extra strength of a hand-cut dovetail is not needed. I use them when I have stacks of drawers to do, for example, for kitchens. Otherwise, I prefer hand-cut dovetails for their strength and looks. Besides, if only a few have to be made, when you've made them for many years you'll find them easier to do than setting up the router.

The through **(14)** and half-blind **(15)** hand dovetails are attractive carcase joints. The full-blind dovetail **(16)** is not used to be "crafty," but is used where strength is important, as in a freestanding cabinet without a back, or in a cabinet with glass doors on both sides, like a showcase.

For joints not at corners, a simple tongue and groove **(17)** can be used for any type of wood except composition board. At the ends of the boards the tongue is set off center so that the outside shoulder isn't too weak.

(18) Fiberboard and particle board are made of waste materials, and so there is no grain strength. Since a tongue would break, a spline must be used with these materials. The spline should go into the carcase side about ⅓ of the side's thickness, and twice that amount into the perpendicular piece. Setting the spline further into the side will weaken it, and keeping it shorter in the perpendicular piece will not add enough strength.

I would never use a fully-housed dado joint **(19)**. There are no shoulders to lock the wood and help resist sideway stresses. Also, if the wood is sanded after the joint is cut, the piece becomes too loose. If there are imperfections in the wood, the piece will not fit tightly.

Another strong joint is a series of small mortises and tenons **(20)**. For extra strength, the tenons should run through the sides and be wedged from the outside at assembly.

The sliding dovetail **(21)** is an excellent joint for perpendiculars. The double-shoulder version is machine-cut with a router and a dovetail bit. The single-shoulder joint is cut by hand with a dovetail plane and its corresponding saw, and with a router plane. The machine version is excellent for production. If only a few sliding dovetails are required, the hand method is preferred. It is extremely simple and much faster than one would expect. In the hand version the track is tapered so that the dovetail slides in easily at first and locks at the end as it is hammered into place. Consequently, as the dovetail is forced in tight, a small shoulder is pressed into the straight side and increases at the narrow end. In the machine version, the pieces should mate exactly and thus require a lot of force to assemble, especially if a long dovetail is glued, because the glue swells the grain, making the piece increasingly difficult to slide in.

With both types of sliding dovetails, glue is not necessary, but a spot of glue should be put at the front to fix it in position, or the whole length can be glued. If two different materials are used (e.g., plywood shelves into solid sides), only the front should be glued so that as movement occurs, the front will remain flush.

In a chest of drawers or similar carcase higher or wider than 2 ft., some sort of strengthening brace will be required. I use a sliding dovetail in the center brace, and if additional bracing is needed, a tongue and groove out to the sides. The sliding dovetail holds the center in tight.

If you wish to keep joints from showing through in front, you can stop the joints before the front or else cover them. In solid wood I sometimes cut a ½-in. strip off the cabinet, run the joints through and reglue the strip. In plywood I run the joints through and add a facing for the same result.   ⊓

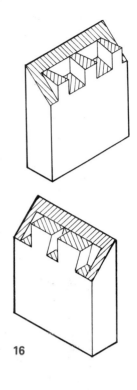

16

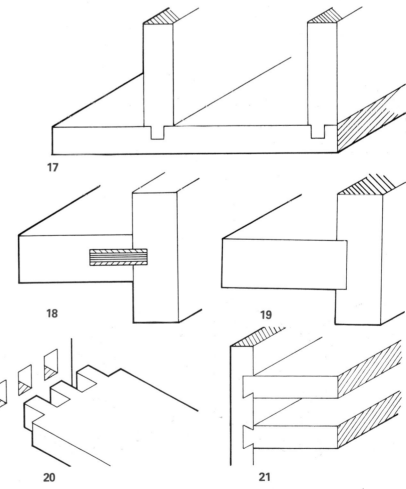

17

18

19

20

21

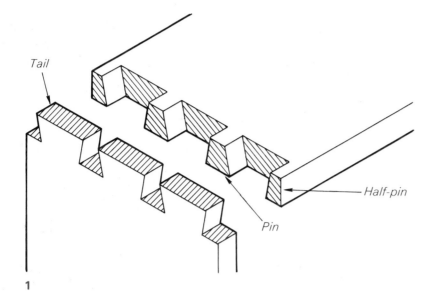

Tail

Half-pin

Pin

1

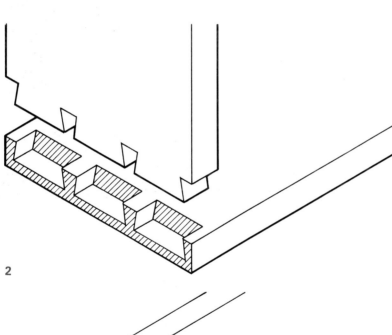

2

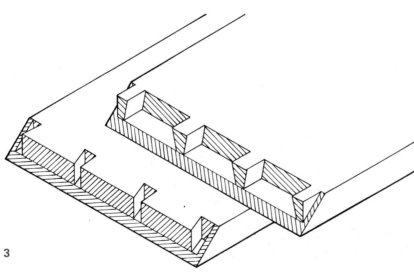

3

Dovetails

The dovetail has been and still is the mark of fine cabinetmaking. Correctly made, a dovetail is a strong and durable joint. It has a decorative effect and adds a sense of strength to a piece.

There are several types of dovetails. In through dovetails **(1)**, both pieces go completely through each other and the joint is visible on the outside surfaces of both pieces. In half-blind dovetails **(2)**, one piece is joined to about two-thirds the thickness of the corresponding piece, and so is visible on only one outside surface. In full-blind dovetails **(3)**, the pieces are mitered at the edges and the pins and tails stop before the miters so the joint is not visible from the outside of either piece.

Specific tools are required to make hand-cut dovetails. The ease of making the joint and the quality of the finished result depend on the correct use of these tools. Each tool must be sharpened to function correctly.

Once the wood has been milled, the pieces cut to size and the edges squared, marking for the joint begins. The first step in making any dovetail is to scribe the depth of the joint with a marking gauge. □

Through Dovetails

For the through dovetail, the full thickness of the wood plus a hair more (about 1/64 in.) has to be set into the marking gauge **(1)**. The extra bit will ensure that the pieces will go all the way through each other **(2)**, and that any excess will come off the pins and tails. It is much easier to sand off this excess. If the gauge were set too low, the whole side would have to be planed or sanded down.

The angle of the dovetail was arrived at a long time ago through experimentation. The angle is about 80°. If the angle were less the tail might slip out; if the angle were greater the wood on the tail would break. Here **(3)** the angle has been exaggerated to show how the wood breaks off. At the extreme points of both parts of the joint the corners are short grain, which breaks easily.

The easiest way to find the angle is to draw a square line across a piece of wood. Divide the line into six equal parts using a ruler or divider. Mark a point to either side of the line the same distance as one part **(4)**. Connect this base point with the top end of the line **(5)** and you should have a triangle, the hypotenuse of which slopes at the correct angle for any kind of dovetail. This is a one-to-six ratio. The angle can be transferred with a sliding bevel to the end of the piece that is to be joined. A sliding bevel is like a square, but the tongue is movable and can angle and slide.

(6) Two types of sliding bevel are shown here. They're both good.

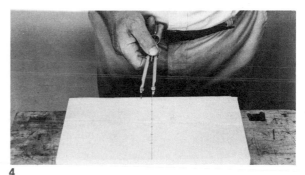

1

2

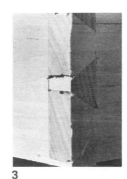

3

4

5

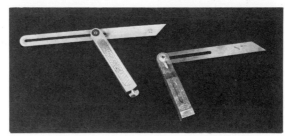

6

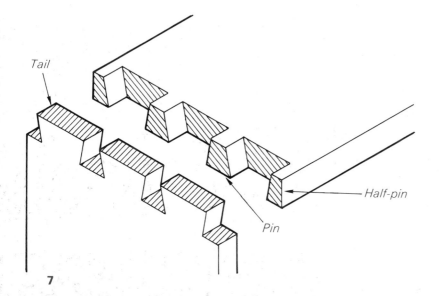

Tail

Half-pin

Pin

7

8

9

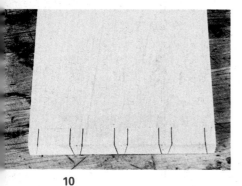

10

11

When making a dovetail, start with the pins. The distance between the pins will vary with the width of the wood, but I would never make their centers more than 3 in. apart. When laying out the pins, start with a half pin on each end (7) because tails get their strength from being glued to pins, not vice versa. A tail at the end would not be properly anchored because that part is an end-grain joint. A half-pin is called a half-pin because it is angled on only one side, not because of its smaller size.

Divide the space between the pins evenly. The way you lay out the spacing depends a lot on personal taste. If you wish, you can achieve some highly decorative effects.

When you first learn to make dovetails, it is a good idea to lay the pins out using a sliding bevel on the ends (8) and a square on the face (9). When you get more proficient, this might not be necessary.

Now the pins are laid out (10). There are different saws to choose from for cutting the dovetails. The only two that I use are the bowsaw and the offset dovetail saw. I use the bowsaw for wood ½ in. or thicker, and the dovetail saw for anything smaller. The bowsaw cuts much faster than any other saw and makes a narrower cut. With any saw, let the saw lie loosely in your hands, and don't apply any pressure. This is especially true when starting the cut. Use your thumb as a guide, keeping the saw to the *waste* side of the line, following or splitting the line (11). Make sure you don't saw below the scribed line depths.

When the pins are cut, the excess is chiseled out with a chisel and mallet. The chisel has to be sharp. Some chisels are manufactured with handles that have rounded ends. I always flatten these out so the mallet won't slide off the end of the handle. The only exception to this is when I am using the chisel as a carving tool, where I would rest the end in the palm of my hand and push with my hand instead of a mallet.

Use a mallet when striking a chisel. If you use a steel hammer, you will flare out the end of a wooden handle. I like lathe-turned mallets (12). They rest in your hand easily and because they are round, they don't have to be used in a specific position.

Once the chisel is sharp, the wood can be removed between the pins. Clean the area of the bench where you will clamp the board to prevent marring the piece. Use a scrap piece of wood between the clamp and the dovetailed piece so that the clamp doesn't leave an impression in the wood. Clamp the wood to the bench, always over a leg so that as you strike the chisel into the piece, the piece will stay firmly seated. If you clamp the piece over the vise, you run the risk of breaking the vise from the force. And the piece will be harder to chisel out, since the vise doesn't provide as much support as a leg.

Use a chisel to cut the marking-gauge line deeper (13), so that when you chisel out the waste, the grain won't break behind the line. Then make a V-cut at the back of the dovetail for the chisel to rest up against (14). If you didn't do this and you didn't set the chisel in just the right spot on the line, the line would be uneven and gaps would show between the two pieces when they were joined.

The back of the joint is undercut slightly (15,16). The end grain does not provide any glue surface. The object is to get a straight line that will be tight when the joint is together. By undercutting, you ensure that the joint will pull in tight and the line between the boards will be closed.

The flat side of the chisel should be away from you (17) when you use the chisel vertically to cut at the back, and should be facing up (18) when you cut in from the ends to remove the waste.

Chisel only about halfway down from each side. Don't try and take too much wood with one cut. Be careful not to tear the edges of the pins when their wide side is up. Go partway down and remove the excess before chiseling down again. When you have chiseled about halfway down, turn the piece over and continue the same way (19,20). This helps eliminate the problem of tearing wood out from beyond the joint. Remember to undercut on each side.

Sometimes there are still small pieces of wood in the corners that will have to be cleaned out (21,22) for the joint to go together tightly.

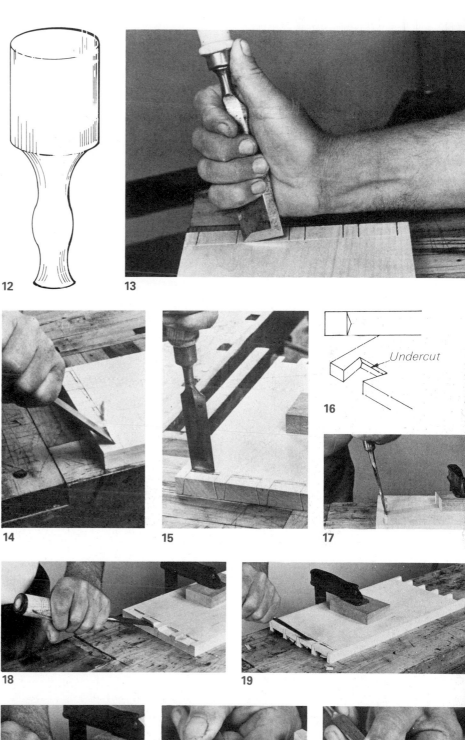

12   13

14   15   16   17

Undercut

18   19

20

21

22

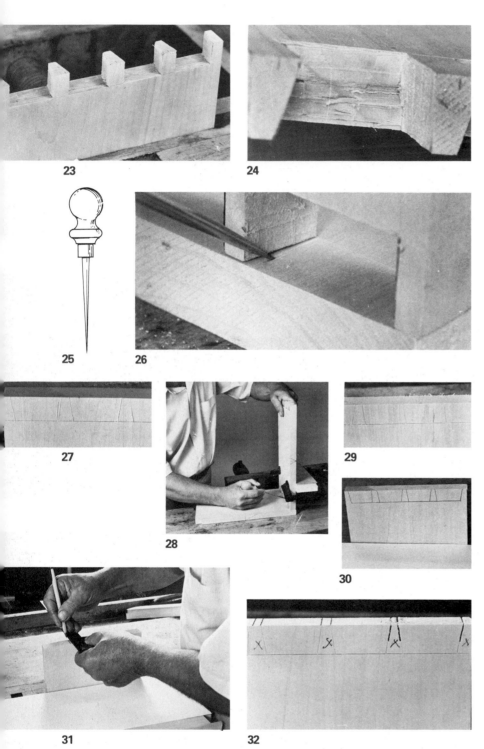

27

28

29

30

31

32

(23) Here is the cleaned-out corner. Note the undercut **(24)** at the back, or bottom, of the joint.

The reason the pins are made first is that it is easier to follow the tail saw line. If the tails were made first and the pins were scribed onto the end of the wood from the tail, the first sawcut on the end grain would destroy the pin line since end-grain fibers become fuzzy so easily. And we all know how difficult it is to follow a line started on end grain. By making the pins first and scribing the tails from them, we can begin sawing on the face side of the wood, and we have more strokes to try to saw the line accurately.

Instead of buying a scriber, I use a scratch awl **(25)** to scribe with. I like the long, slim awl better, and I don't have to buy another tool. If the end of the awl doesn't come to a smooth, sharp point, the line will move away from the pin. Never use a pencil to transfer lines. It is not accurate enough. (In this book I sometimes use a pencil so the lines will show up in the photographs.) The sharp point of the awl breaks the fibers along the line, making a crisp, clean mark.

Always scribe from the inside of the pieces. If you scribe from the outside, as in the picture **(26)**, the point of the scriber will tend to move away from the pin and follow a grain line instead. Scribing from the inside helps force the scriber up against the pin.

The scribed lines should show clearly. On the second pin from the right in the photograph **(27)** you can see where the scriber followed the grain instead of the pin (when scribed from the outside).

(28) The correct way to scribe is to hold the piece with the pins, putting enough pressure on it so it will not slip. Later, when making half-blind and full-blind dovetails, you'll have to scribe from the inside—you'll have no choice. This picture also shows you what to do if the piece warps. By clamping a board across the width you will straighten it out enough to mark it accurately to the other piece.. Once the joint is cut and glued together, the board will stay straight. To prevent marring the surface with clamps, you should always use blocks of wood. I didn't, for clarity.

If the scribed lines are hard to see **(29)** place a piece of white cardboard, or even better, a mirror, in front of the piece **(30)**. The light will be reflected back up and the scribed lines will appear as shadows. This can be a great aid when you begin to saw the tails.

You can also mark the square lines across the end grain using a square **(31)**. This isn't necessary, but will serve as an added guide when you saw the lines.

One common mistake people make when first cutting dovetails is that they try to cut the tails a little oversized so they can fit them later by paring them to size with a chisel. This is a bad practice. It is very time-consuming to fit the tails by chiseling and filing them, and it is much easier and faster to learn to saw them correctly in the first place. When you do learn to cut them right and everything fits correctly the first time, you might be surprised. It does take practice. But through this practice, you will gain both self-confidence and experience with the tools, both of which will help making any joint that much easier. The secret to making joints that fit, whether you are making them by hand or machine, is to learn to split the scribed line in half, and always to keep the sawcut to the waste side of the line. The tails can even be cut on a band saw. The principle is the same: Stay to the waste side of the line and both pieces will go together perfectly.

(32) This cut was stopped partway down to show that the thickness of the sawblade is on the waste side (marked with *x*'s) of the line. The cut just splits the line in half.

(33) Here, the sawcut on the right has gone below the scribed line. This cut will show when the joint is together. The cut on the left is on the wrong side of the line.

(34,35) The tails are cleaned out exactly like the pins, but with the opposite sections chiseled out and using a smaller chisel. Undercut except at the ends.

(36) It is advisable to mark the square lines for the cuts that will saw off the end spaces for the half-pins. Then saw out the two pieces **(37)**. Don't undercut here as this edge will be visible. Again, be sure the corners are clean **(38)**.

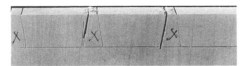

33

34

35

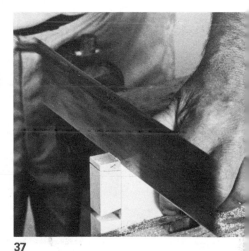

36

37

38

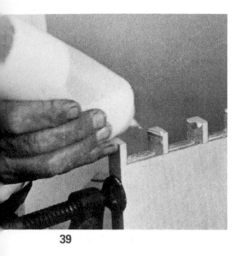

39

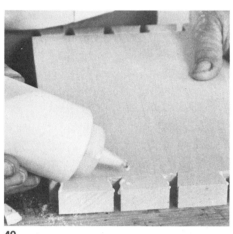

40

41

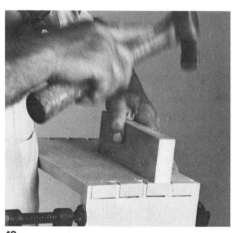

42

43

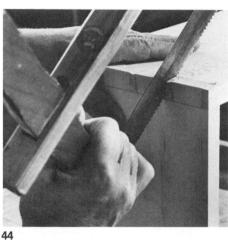

44

45

44

46

Be sure to sand the inside of the boards before gluing up. Once the pieces are assembled it will be difficult to sand to the inside corners.

Before gluing, you'll want to dry-test your joints, but it is not a good idea to put the joints fully together. Doing so may make the joint sloppy and may even break it. Just check to see if everything fits. Then glue it together and hope. When you glue the pieces, squeeze just a little bit of glue on the top of the pins **(39)** and on the inside edges of the tails **(40)**. As the joint slides together, the glue will be pushed ahead of it. (Of course I would glue up all four sides of a cabinet together at once, not one corner only as in this demonstration.) Use a clamp on the side of the piece with the pins **(41)** to prevent splitting if the joint is too tight.

(42) Use a block of wood to hammer on when joining the pieces. This will prevent splitting and marking up the piece. If the joint fits right, it should not be necessary to use clamps. As you are gluing it up, check to see that the pieces are square.

Whenever I make a dovetail there is no doubt in my mind that it is going to go together. This is because I make the pins first, scribe them carefully to the tails, and make sure to split the line when cutting the tails. If I can split the line, and I usually can, the joint has to go together. It is that simple.

If one of the pins or tails is slightly loose, the end grain can be hit with a steel hammer, just enough to flare out the fibers **(43)**. This should be done when you are gluing up the pieces.

If for some reason a part of the dovetail does not fit at all, saw a cut a little thinner than the thickness of veneer down the line between the pin and the tails **(44,45)**.

(46) Cut and **(47)** hammer a piece of veneer (preferably against a piece of steel) to compress the grain, or squeeze it in a steel vise to flatten it out. Cut the piece of veneer at 45° so that the grain will run in the same direction as the pins.

When applying the glue, rub it into the sawcut using your finger to force it in deep. Don't put glue on the veneer or it will swell up before it is inserted. When inserted **(48)**, the veneer will pick up some moisture from the glue and will expand to fit the slot perfectly. Be sure to choose a piece of veneer — or if you make your own, a piece of wood — that has the same color as the pin.

When the glue is dry, the veneers sawn off **(49)**, and the piece is sanded, no one will see the patch. The marked areas **(50)** show where the veneer was inserted and sanded off. You notice it only if it is brought to your attention. Sometimes, with a perfect color match, it is impossible to see.

If I am making several sets of dovetails, I stack up all the pieces for the pins and chisel them all out at once **(51,52)**, scribe each joint to its corresponding piece and then stack up all the tails and chisel them all at once. This saves considerable time. □

47

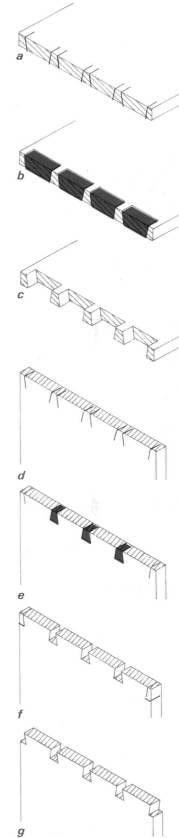

a

b

c

d

e

f

g

48

49

50

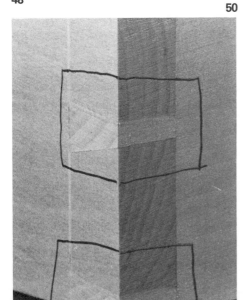

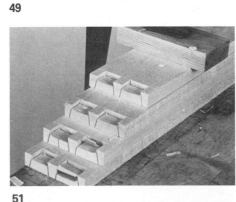

51

52

1

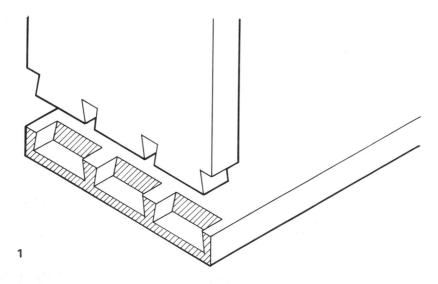

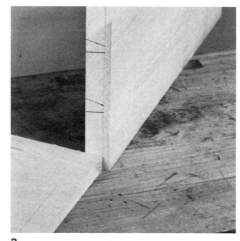

2

3

4

5

Half-Blind Dovetails

A half-blind dovetail **(1)** is used primarily where you want only one side of the joint to show. It is often used to join drawer fronts to sides. In that case, you usually don't want to see the joint on the front of the drawer, but a nicely made dovetail would look fine on the drawer side. With drawers, the sides are usually thinner than the front. Half-blind dovetails can be used for pieces of different thicknesses or for pieces of the same thickness.

Here, pieces of different thickness are being joined. If this were a drawer the pins would be in the thicker piece (the drawer front), and the tails in the thinner piece (the side). The side must be flush with the end of the front. Using an awl, mark the full thickness of the side onto the front piece **(2)**, then scribe with a marking gauge. The depth of the pin should be about two-thirds the thickness of the front So set the marking gauge to that depth and mark the ends of the front, and with the same setting, mark the sides. Then lay out the pins exactly as when making through dovetails **(3)**.

To saw out the pins, hold the saw at an angle **(4)** so that it cuts only between the two scribed lines on the edge and front.

An old scraper blade or sawblade completes the cut. Make sure the scraper isn't sharp so it doesn't split the wood. Hammer the blade down **(5)** until it reaches the bottom corner of the cut. Pop it out **(6)** by hitting the underside upwards with the hammer.

(7) Chisel out the excess the same way as in a through dovetail (see p. 67), but of course, you can work from only one side. Chisel down to the marked line on the end of the front piece.

(8) Clean the rest of the wood out, and again, undercut.

(9) Be sure the corners are cleaned out.

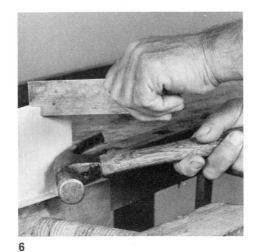

6

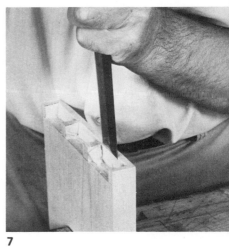

7

8

10

11

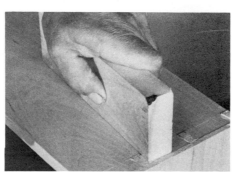

12

(10) To lay out the tails, scribe them from the pins, making sure the board with the pins is offset to make the inside edge flush with the marking-gauge line since these are not through dovetails. Cut and chisel the tails the same way as in through dovetails.

(11) When the joint is completed, tap it together lightly to check the fit. Use a block of wood for better protection.

(12) Don't work it all the way down until you are gluing it up. ☐

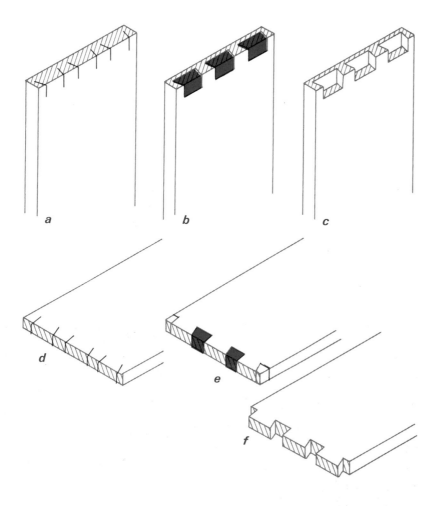

a

b

c

d

e

f

Full-Blind Dovetails

Most people think it is difficult to make a full-blind dovetail **(1)**. It looks complicated, but it is not. If you can make the through and half-blind versions, you should have no trouble making the full-blind dovetail. The only difference is that when you lay it out, you have to set the marking gauge to the exact thickness of the wood so that the ends will meet in a clean miter. In laying out through dovetails, we set the marking gauge slightly bigger than the thickness of the wood to make sure the ends of the joint protrude so they could be sanded off. Here, the depth must be set exactly right. Otherwise, the joint will not be tight on the inside or outside.

To begin the joint, you must first rabbet the ends of both boards **(2)**. This is most easily done on a table saw. If you do it by hand, you can use a rabbet plane **(3,4)**. There are some very fancy rabbet planes available,

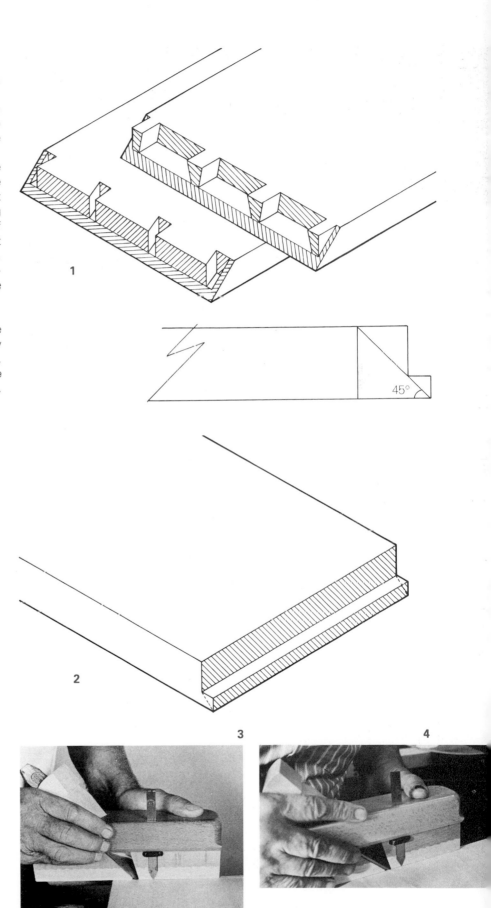

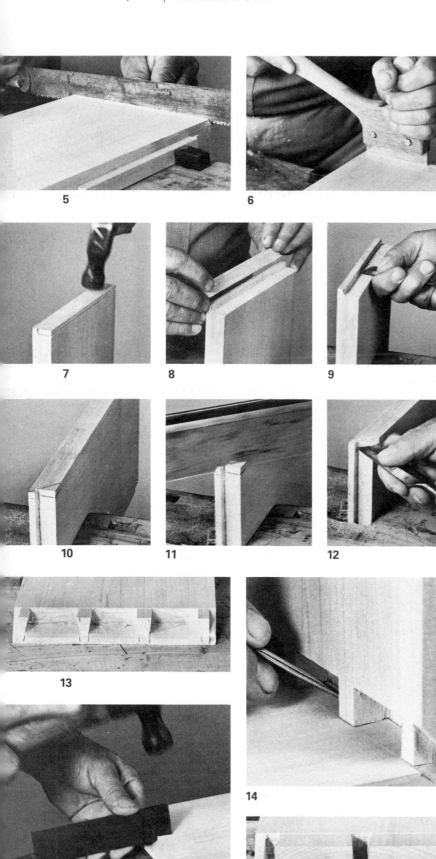

5

6

7

8

9

10

11

12

13

14

15

16

but I prefer a simple one. Or you can saw off the excess with a handsaw. I prefer to use a bowsaw **(5)** if the piece is not too wide. If it is very wide I use a saw designed for making sliding dovetails **(6)**. In either case I make a half *V*-groove for the saw to rest in and get it started accurately. Refer to the section on sliding dovetails (p. 140) for more on the dovetail saw and plane.

After making the cut, use a sharp marking gauge to scribe the end of the rabbet on the end grain. The piece should come out easily with just a light tap with a hammer **(7,8)**.

(9) Be sure the corner is clean. Rabbet out the other piece in exactly the same manner.

To cut the end miters, mark both the front and back and the corners to 45° **(10)**. On a ¾-in. piece, the miter should be about ¼ in. wide—just enough thickness to hide the joint.

(11) Saw, then **(12)** chisel out the angles on both pieces, pins and tails.

When that is done, lay out and saw the pins the same way as in half-blind dovetails (see p. 72). Again, use the scraper blade to complete the cut. Then chisel out the pins **(13)**.

(14) Use the pins to scribe the tails, as in half-blind dovetails. But cutting the tails differs slightly. Here they can only be cut halfway as in making the pins, because the saw is angled. **(15)** The scraper blade again finishes off the cut.

After the waste is chiseled out, the tails are done **(16)**.

17

With both the pins and tails completed, only the miters along the long edge need to be cut. This is most easily done on the table saw. When there are only a few, I cut them by hand with a sharp chisel **(17)** or with a rabbet plane. If you use a rabbet plane **(18)** don't run the plane the whole length in the final cuts. Come in backwards at the end **(19)** so that you don't sliver it off. You could also cut the miter along the edge before cutting the dovetail, as shown in the sequential drawing below.

(20) The pieces are ready to go together. Here I would work them together all the way **(21)** to make sure they fit.

If the corner is slightly open, check that all the corners are cleaned out. If there is still a slight opening, hit the edge lightly with a hammer **(22)** when you are gluing up. This will bend over the fibers and close the imperfection. Here you see the correction almost completed **(23)**   □

18

19

20

21

22

23

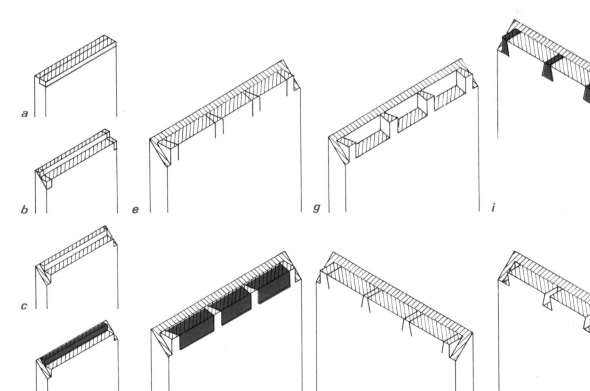

a

b

c

d

e

f

g

h

i

j

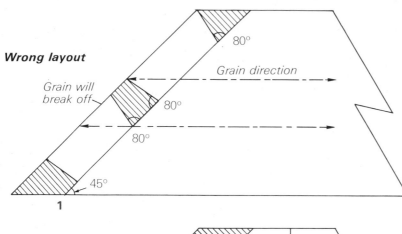

Wrong layout

80°

Grain direction

Grain will break off

80°

80°

45°

1

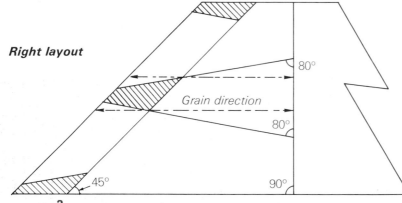

Right layout

80°

Grain direction

80°

45°

90°

2

3

Hand Dovetails with Compound Miter

Through hand dovetails on boards that meet at a compound angle (as in a pyramid) are very difficult to make. It is a good idea to practice on some scrap pieces before cutting the actual joint. Here, I'm making a 45° joint—the steepest angle I would dovetail. But before making this joint, be sure you can make a 90° through dovetail (see pp. 65-71).

The pins are laid out differently from the regular or square dovetail joint. The drawing **(1)** shows the wrong way to lay out the pins. Here the pins are positioned at 80° to the surface, as in a regular dovetail.

This drawing **(2)** shows the right way to lay out the pins. First draw a square line across the board, and mark the pins 80° from that mark.

To make a compound-mitered dovetail, tilt the sawblade 45° (in this case) and cut the top and bottom edges at 45°, the angle the pyramid sides make with the base **(3)**. (For a steeper 60° pyramid, the blade would be set at 60°.) Others may find it less confusing to cut these edges *after* the compound miter is cut.

To cut the ends off, so the pyramid sides meet properly, tilt the sawblade and set the miter gauge to the correct angle using the table provided **(4)**. In this case, the sawblade is set to 30° and the miter gauge at 54¾°. Cut some scrap pieces first and check if the two pieces are square when put together.

Table Saw Settings for Compound Dovetails

Tilt of Sides (from Vertical)	Table-Saw Tilt (from Vertical)	Miter-Gauge Angle (from Sawblade)
5°	½°	85°
10°	1½°	80¼°
15°	3¾°	75½°
20°	6¼°	71¼°
25°	10°	67°
30°	14½°	63½°
35°	19½°	60¼°
40°	24½°	57¼°
45°	30°	54¾°
50°	36°	52½°
55°	42°	50¾°
60°	48°	49°

4

(5) When everything is set correctly, make the first cut with the miter gauge in the groove on the left side of the sawblade.

(6) For the second cut, move the miter gauge to the groove on the right side of the sawblade, but use the miter gauge backwards. Or you could screw a piece of wood to the miter gauge long enough to reach beyond the sawblade when the miter gauge is in the groove on the right side of the blade (in which case the miter gauge is not used backwards). Don't change the angle of the sawblade or the angle of the miter gauge. If the piece is too wide, a plywood jig could be used (see p. 124).

(7) Mark the pins for the depth of the dovetails.

(8) Because the ends are angled, a marking gauge cannot be used.

(9) Set the bevel at the correct angle, and **(10)** scribe the line with a knife.

(11) Transfer the line to the other side of the board by squaring over the line, and use the bevel again.

When you lay out the pins at the end of the board, take the two different angles from the drawing **(12)**, but remember to hold the bevel gauge against the 45° line. When marking the pins on the end of the board, have the bevel square to the surface because the bevel was flat on the drawing when it was set **(13)**.

(14) Set the bevel so it is parallel with the edges when marking down the pins **(15)**.

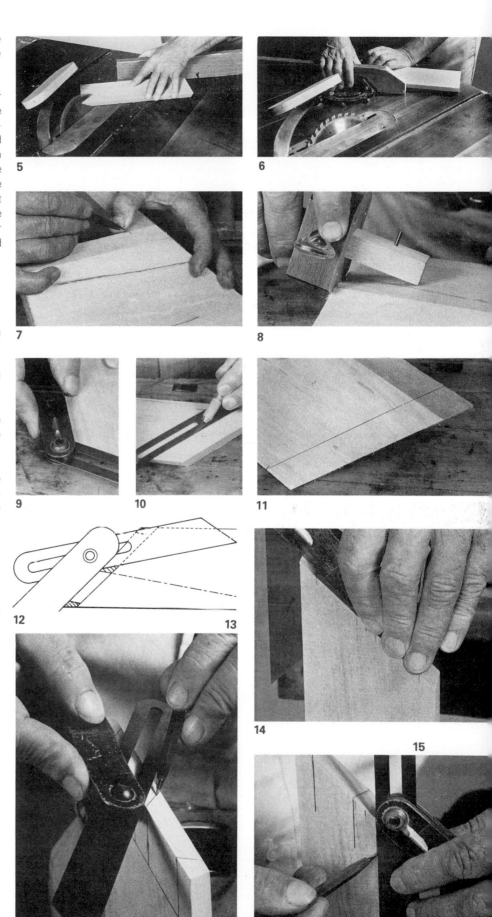

5

6

7

8

9

10

11

12

13

14

15

16

17

18

19

20

21

22

(16) Now the pins are laid out, ready to be cut and chiseled.

After the pins are chiseled out, double-check that the pins are parallel with the outside edges so that when the joint slides together, splitting won't occur **(17)**.

(18) Now scribe the tails from the pins.

On the end of the piece with the tails, set the bevel at the same angle as the edges **(19)** and mark them across **(20)**.

(21) The tails are marked and ready to be cut. Cut the tails a little oversized so final fitting can be done with a sharp chisel. This is one of the few times I fit the tails with a chisel, because I have found it's very difficult to cut accurately.

(22) The joint, glued together and sanded. □

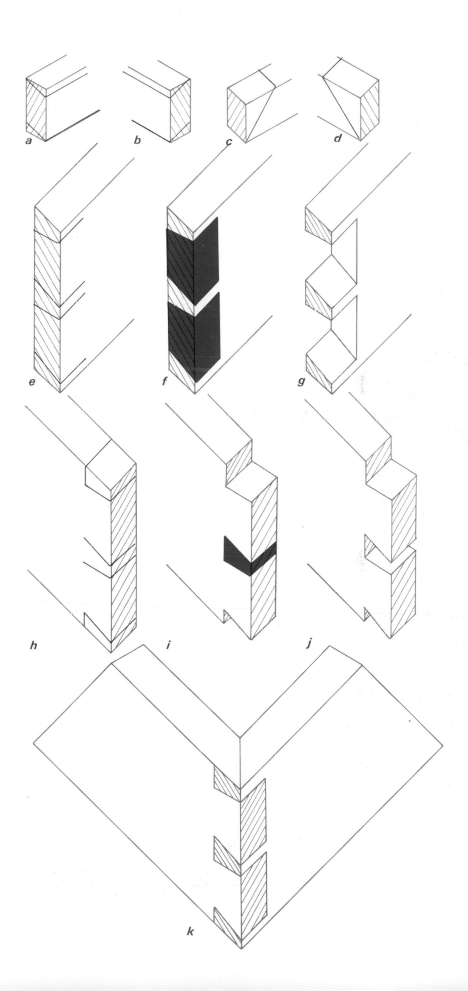

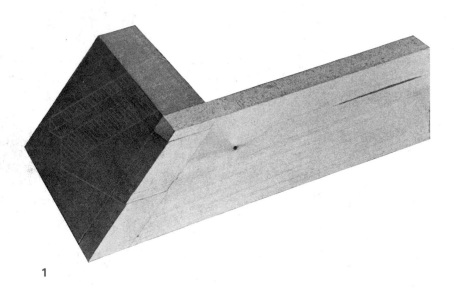

1

Simple-Angled Dovetails

(1) These dovetails are cut at an angle of 45°, but one side is square. This joint is a little easier to make than the compound dovetail, especially if the pins are in the piece with the angle on the end, as shown here. The pins are cut 80° from the surface, as in straight dovetailing, and parallel to the outside edges, as for compound-angled dovetails (see pp. 78-81). □

Routing Dovetails

A router is one of the most important electric hand tools in the shop, so when buying one, don't try to save a few dollars, but get a good one with at least a 1-hp motor. Make sure the mechanics that move the router up and down in the base are easy to work and accurate. Check where the switch is located, and if it is easy to turn on and off while routing. And get a router that can take both ¼-in. and ½-in. bits. Don't try to make a router do double duty as a planer using special attachments. The few times you need it it's easier to plane by hand.

The router can be used to make half-blind dovetails, a very strong joint that is easy to make once the jig is set up. I don't think machine dovetails look as good as handcut dovetails, but because of the strength of the joint and the short time required to make them, I always use machine dovetails for a drawer or for anything where strength is needed and the joint won't be exposed.

(1) A special jig has to be used with the router, and it can be used to make only half-blind dovetails. Of the several types of jigs on the market, all seem to work well. When you consider the time that will be saved, these jigs are a good investment. They are especially useful if you plan to make a quantity of drawers, small boxes or the like, where a router-made dovetail would be a good choice for a joint. Buy the widest jig you can find. The price won't be much higher and you will have the added flexibility of being able to work with wider pieces.

I am not going to describe all the adjustments and parts of the jig you will have to set up. When you buy a jig (sometimes called a machine dovetail template) it will come with a full description with all the particulars for that jig.

Different-sized finger templates **(2)** will be available for most jigs. I would buy a ½-in. for larger work, and a ¼-in. one for smaller work. You will also need template guides that attach to the router base and fit into the finger templates, and the correct-size dovetail router bits **(3)**. Be sure the template guide and accessories will work

1

2

3

4

5

6

7

8

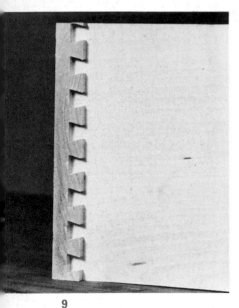

9

10

with your particular router — they are usually not interchangeable.

(4) The two boards are placed at right angles to each other, offset by the width of a pin. The whole operation is very simple. Just let the template guide follow the fingers on the template **(5)**. The pins and the tails are both made at the same time.

This picture **(6)** shows the pins and tails after they are cut.

(7) Here the finger template is removed. Notice the offset between the two boards, which is equal to half the distance between the fingers or pins. To put the boards together, the top board is aligned and flipped 180° towards the camera.

(8) By moving the finger template back and forth, the depth of the dovetail can be adjusted to make the dovetails flush, or to make the pins sit deeper, as in a lipped drawer.

In this example **(9)** the finger template was moved back ⅛ in. from the flush position to make a ¼-in. lip. Moving the template ⅛ in. back makes the pins ⅛ in. deeper and the tails ⅛ in. thinner, so do it only where the side is at least ½ in. thick. The dovetails are cut first, and the lip is cut out after they are completed **(10)**.

A disadvantage of using machine dovetails is that you may not always finish with a half-pin if you are limited to a particular dimension. This has nothing to do with the strength, only the looks. If the depth of the drawer or piece is not critical, the pieces could be dimensioned to finish off with a half-pin. In photo **(9)**, the pin at the end is very small. Here, I planned to cut the pieces to size later, finishing with a half-pin. The dimensions were not critical. □

Making Dovetails on a Table Saw

Dovetails can be made on the circular saw with a variation of the miter-gauge jig used for making finger joints (see p. 90). Because small errors tend to accumulate, you have to be sure the spacing is precise when you make dovetails by machine. Lay the pins out the same way you would for hand-cut dovetails (see pp.65-66).

(1) Put in a dado blade about ⅜ in. thick and raise the blade to a little more than the thickness of the wood the tails will be made from.

The first cut to be made will be the half-pin. Fasten a ¾-in. piece of plywood to the miter gauge and set the gauge at 80° — the angle for dovetails — and pass it over the dado blade **(2)**.

Clamp a wood stop **(3)** to this plywood jig so that you can make the same cut in all the pieces that will have pins.

Unscrew the jig from the miter gauge. Make a guide pin insert that fits snugly into the slot and glue it in **(4)**. It should be a couple of inches long.

Return the jig to the miter gauge. Clamp, but don't screw it on yet because you have to adjust now for the distance between pins. Put the slot from the first cut over the guide pin in the jig.

(5) Set the next cut according to your layout for the dovetail pins, being sure to skip one line, which will have the opposite angle. When the blade is in the correct position, clamp the jig to the miter gauge and then screw it on. It is advisable to check all cuts on a test joint (made with scrap wood the same size as the finished stock) to see that everything is set up correctly. Make all the cuts across the piece using the cut for the first pin as a starting point and moving to the right for each cut. Remember to skip every other line, since these will be cut at the opposite angle.

1

2

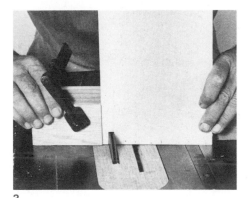
3

4

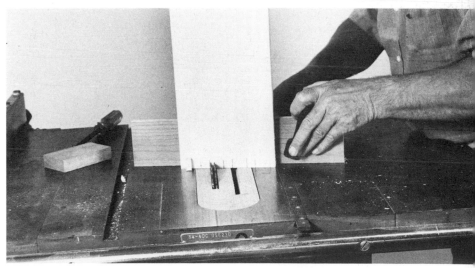
5

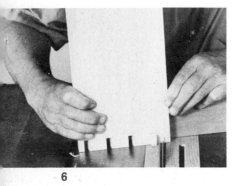

6

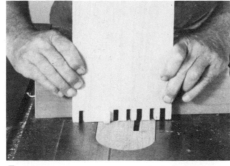

7

8

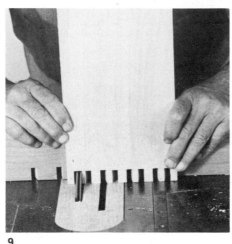

9

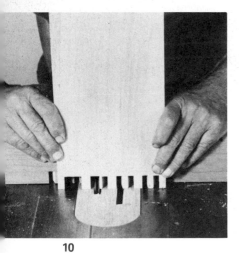

10

11

(6) When these cuts are made, change the miter gauge to 80° in the opposite direction and repeat the procedures so you can cut the other side of the pins. The jig will have to be reset according to your layout. Again, test on scrap first.

(7) Make the rest of the cuts, this time moving to the left. This will complete the sawing of the pins **(8)**. All the pins are the same size and the same distance apart. All the pieces are thus interchangeable.

(9,10) Now set the miter gauge to 90° and remove the excess wood between the pins. If the dado blades are not sharpened perfectly, it may be necessary to clean along the end grain with a chisel. **(11)** This completes the pins.

To cut the tails, use a sawblade instead of the dado head. Great care has to be taken when cutting the tails to be sure they will fit the pins. Tilt the arbor 10° and set the miter gauge at 90°. Check the angle of the pins with a bevel **(12)** to see that they correspond to the setting of the blade **(13)**.

(14) Make the first cut in all the pieces that will have tails. Use a stop so that all cuts are accurate. The first cut must fit the first cut of the half-pin.

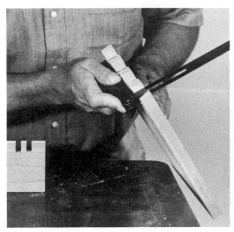

12

13

14

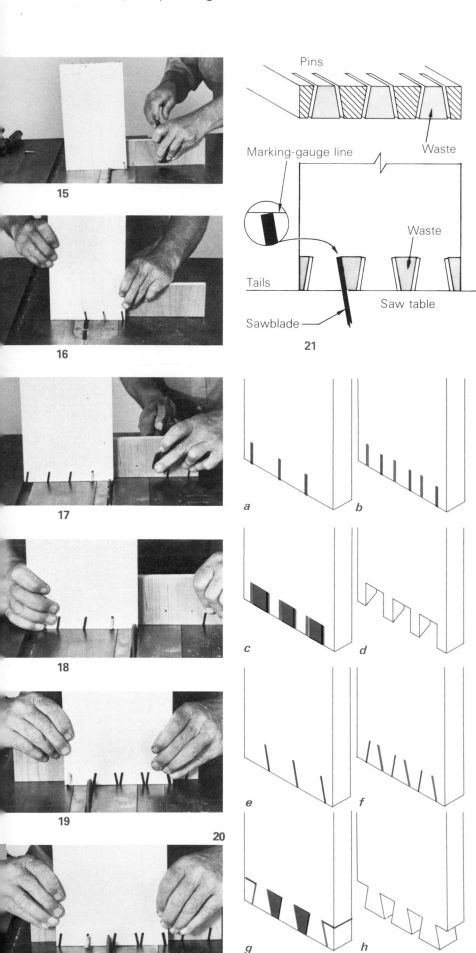

15

16

17

18

19

20

Pins

Marking-gauge line

Waste

Waste

Tails

Saw table

Sawblade

21

a

b

c

d

e

f

g

h

With the first cut made, insert a guide pin. The pin should fit snugly into the cut. Move the fence on the miter gauge so the guide pin is to the left of the blade. Align the piece for the second cut, and when correct, screw the jig on **(15)**. Using a scrap piece, make the first few cuts **(16)** and check the piece against the pins to see if your setting is right before cutting your final piece.

When all first cuts for the tails have been made, the jig on the miter gauge has to be moved for the second cut on the tails. Move it and flip it so the guide pin is on the right side of the blade and tilted in the opposite direction **(17)**.

(18) At the same time, the piece to be cut has to be turned 180° because the table saw tilts only one way.

(19) With the guide pin inserted in what was the last cut and is now the first cut (since the piece was turned around) set the jig for the next cut. When correctly set, screw the jig on and make the cut. Again, it is a good idea to check the setting on your scrap piece before making the cut on the final piece.

(20) Continue this way to cut the tails.

(21) Because the circular-saw blade makes a square cut at the top of the tooth, and because the blade is tilted, the corners can not be cleaned by machine. To remove the wood between the tails, use a chisel the same way as you would by hand (see p. 66-67). This ensures that the corners will be clean.

Cutting dovetails on a circular saw is very useful when you have a lot of dovetails to cut. It is considerably faster once you have made the setup. And you can be sure that all the pieces will be exactly the same. The pieces are interchangeable so you don't have to keep track. If you are working on a very wide piece, I suggest you make just the pins by machine and then continue the tails by hand. On a wide piece, if you are off just a little, the mistake will compound itself by the end. ☐

Other Multiple Joints
Chapter 6

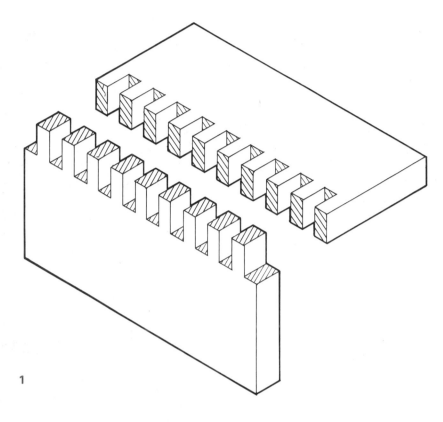

1

Finger Joints

The finger joint, or box joint **(1)**, is the closest machine-made joint to a through dovetail. The great number of pins and the resulting total glue surface make it stronger than a through dovetail. It is easier to make, and just as attractive. The only drawback with this joint is that clamps usually have to be used when gluing it up.

Setting up to make a finger joint is a simple job, and cutting the joint requires no special skills. How well the joint fits depends solely on how accurate the jig is. Trying to make one the first time may be a very frustrating experience, but after a few times it will become very easy.

Once you have the setup, you can make as many joints as you want. To make finger joints you will need a dado head. The size of the cut depends on the width of the board. When deciding, make sure that you will have a full cut at the last slot. Appearance is another important consideration: There should be a harmonious relationship between the pins and the thickness of the wood.

To make the joint, put in the table saw a dado-blade assembly as thick as you want each finger to be. Set the height of the blades a little higher than the thickness of the wood you'll be joining. For a jig, you'll be using a piece of plywood (at least ¾ in.) attached to your miter gauge. If you've used the jig before, make sure the slot in the plywood jig is not higher than the slot to be cut in the pieces or the cuts will tear in the back of the pieces you are joining. Variations on this type of jig will be used for making many other joints on the table saw.

(2) Starting with a fresh jig, make the first cut in the piece of ¾-in. plywood using the dado blades. The dimensions of the board are not critical; neither is the position of the slot. The miter gauge is set at 90°. Plywood is used instead of solid wood for the jig so that the piece between the two sawcuts will be stronger.

Make a guide pin out of a piece of wood the size of the slot and a few inches longer. It should fit snugly into the slot. Choose a hard wood such as maple so that the guide pin will withstand a lot of use.

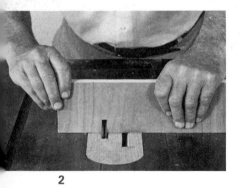

2

3

4

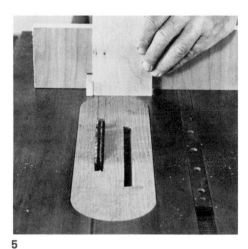

5

With the saw turned off, place the guide pin up against the dado head. Move the plywood on the miter gauge so that the next cut will be precisely one thickness of the guide pin over from the first cut **(3)**.

Clamp the plywood to the miter gauge so that it won't slip while you are screwing it on. Try the jig on two scrap pieces to check the fit. If the joint is too tight, move the plywood so that the first cut is closer to the dado blade. If too loose, move the first cut away from the blade to make the pins bigger. If the fit is correct the joint will slide together easily when tapped with a hammer. If the joint is too tight, each pin will swell a little as glue is applied and the pieces will never go together.

(4) Once the jig is positioned, screw it to the miter gauge and glue in the guide pin.

(5) For the first cut, place the wood tight up against the guide pin. This piece will start out with a pin.

After the first cut is made, move the piece over the guide pin to make the second cut. Proceed in this way until all the slots have been cut **(6)**.

(7) On the matching piece, make the first cut by just covering up the cut for the first slot in the plywood. This piece will then begin with a slot to match the pin in the first cut of the other piece. Hold the piece tightly, because dado blades tend to push the wood to one side. Continue the cuts across the board.

(8,9) The joint is now ready to assemble.

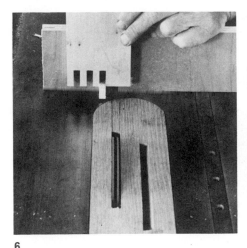

6

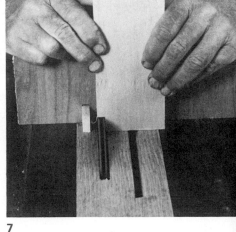

7

8

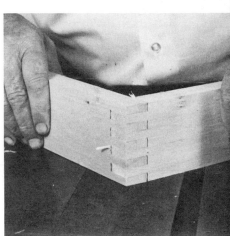

9

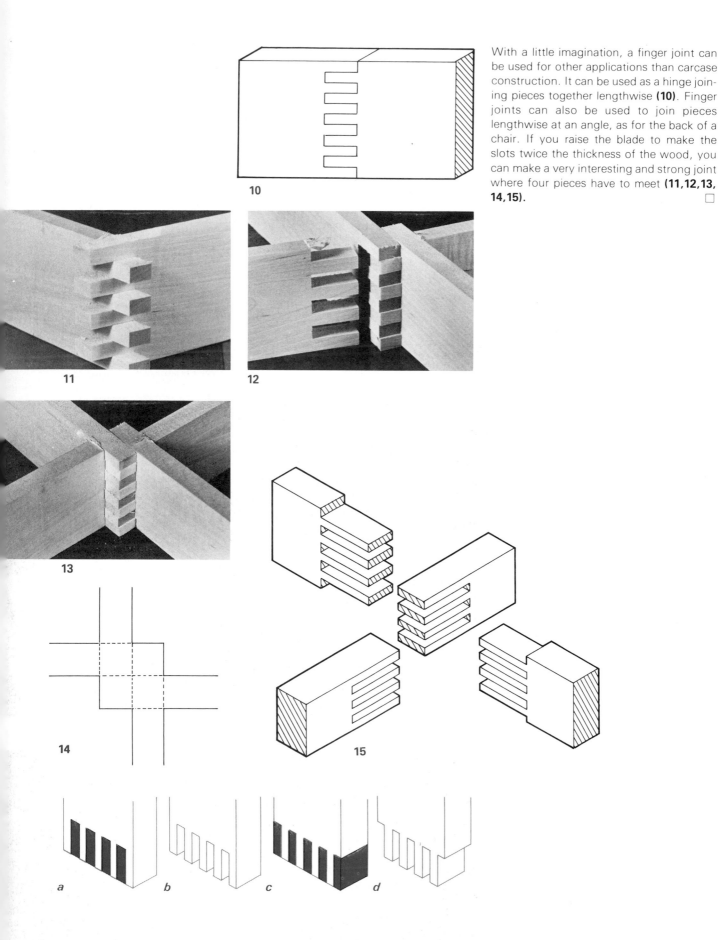

With a little imagination, a finger joint can be used for other applications than carcase construction. It can be used as a hinge joining pieces together lengthwise **(10)**. Finger joints can also be used to join pieces lengthwise at an angle, as for the back of a chair. If you raise the blade to make the slots twice the thickness of the wood, you can make a very interesting and strong joint where four pieces have to meet **(11,12,13, 14,15)**. ☐

10

11

12

13

14

15

a   b   c   d

Angled Finger Joints

To make finger joints at an angle **(1)**, the setup is the same as for making them square, except that the jig screwed to the miter gauge is cut at an angle **(2)**, and so the ends of the boards to be joined are cut at the same angle.

(3) The joint, finished and sanded.   ☐

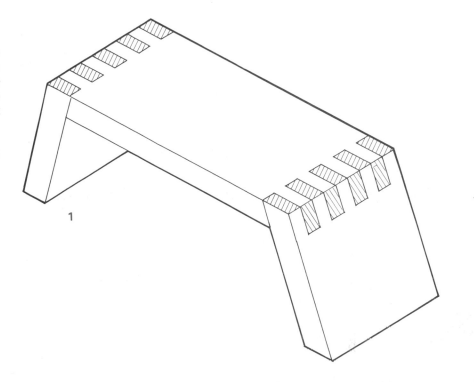

1

2

3

1

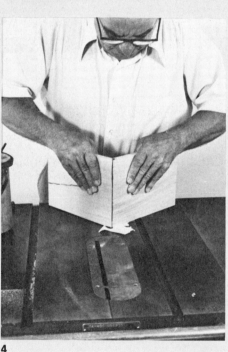

3   4

Hot Glue

Hot glue is good if you need quick setting time. It is made from hides, bones, blood, etc. It can be bought in dry sheets, crust, or as pearls. In whatever form, it has to be soaked in water to soften it. When the glue is soft, pour off any excess water. Put the glue into a double boiler or a glue pot. A glue pot is a double boiler with a thermostat, which keeps the glue from boiling. Never put the pot directly on the heat—it should always be over a pot of water. If hot glue boils it loses its strength. Plus, when it boils it doesn't smell like roses!

When starting a new batch of glue, the best thing after it has softened in water is to melt it. Let it cool, and reheat it again and it will be ready to use. Getting the right consistency is something you have to learn through experimenting. If the glue is hot all day, it will thicken and you'll have to thin it by adding more water. If the consistency is just right, the glue should drop from the brush like heavy maple syrup **(1)**.

The best way to check if the glue is made correctly and ready to use is to put a drop between your fingers **(2)**. Rub your fingers together, applying some pressure. You should be able to squeeze out all the excess easily. After about a minute, depending on the room temperature (if it is 60° F, one minute should be about right), your fingers should start sticking together, because when hot glue gets cold it starts binding. But the glue will never reach its full strength until it dries completely—about 24 hours. Under normal conditions you should be able with care to work with the piece after about two hours.

We all know how hard it is to glue two 45°-cut pieces together if there is no spline or no other part to the joint. Since hot glue sticks when cold, we can glue the two pieces together quickly without clamping. **(3)** Spread the hot glue on both pieces. **(4)** Have paper under the joint so it won't stick to the table. Rub the pieces together hard enough to squeeze out excess glue. The pieces will slide easily at first until the excess is squeezed out. Then it will be hard to move them. Force them together making sure the corners line up, and check for squareness. Leave the pieces about five minutes, then set them aside to dry. ☐

Mock Finger Joints, Cut by Machine

To make the mock finger joint **(1)**, first miter the ends at 45° as if you were making full-blind multiple splines (see p. 110). Then glue the corners together using hot glue (see preceding page). Because the carcase has to be glued up before cutting the mock fingers, this joint is better suited to fairly small carcases that can be easily maneuvered on top of a table saw.

To make the jig for cutting the slots for the splines, use a piece of wood (any kind will do) about 2 in. thick by at least 8 in. wide by 12 in. long. Make sure the two sides are parallel. Tilt the saw to 45° and make the first sawcut **(2)**, running the edge of the piece against the fence. (The fence is on the left side of the saw.)

(3) For the second cut, turn the piece around and reset the fence so the two cuts meet exactly in the bottom of a V-cut **(4)**.

Turn the sawblade back to 90°. Put in the dado blade. In this case I wanted the splines to be ¼ in. thick, so two ⅛-in. dado blades were used. Raise the dado blade so that it will cut as high as possible without coming through on the other corner of the joint or the top of the jig **(5)**.

(6) Make a first cut, holding the jig against the miter gauge. Then cut a spline that fits tightly into the cut.

Decide what distance you want between the splines, and make your second cut with the jig screwed to the miter gauge **(7,8)**. If you make the thickness of the spline and the space between the splines equal, the joint will get its maximum strength and look most like a true finger joint.

1

2

3

4

5

6

7

8

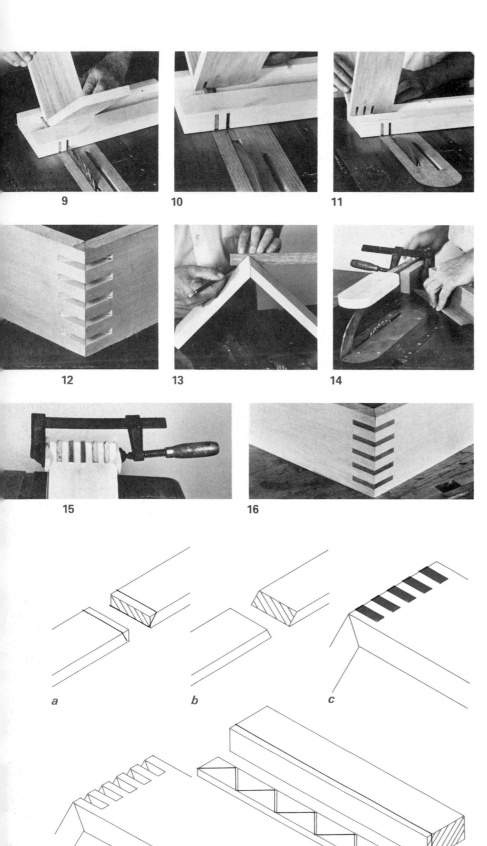

9

10

11

12

13

14

15

16

a

b

c

d

e

(9) Hold the carcase piece to be joined against the guide spline or pin in the first cut in the jig, and make the first cut in the piece.

(10) After the first cut is made, move the piece so the cut fits over the guide pin. Make the second cut.

(11) Continue down the pieces until all the cuts are made **(12)**.

Make the splines exactly the same way as described in multiple spline joints (see pp. 105-107). Insert the splines and mark them for size **(13)**. Make them about ⅛ in. wider than needed.

(14) Set the miter gauge at 45°, and cut the splines as described in half and full-blind multiple splines. Make sure the splines are slightly longer, say ³⁄₃₂ in., than they need to be. Then they can be sanded down to create a smooth joint.

(15) When gluing in the splines, be sure to put the glue in the slots and not on the splines. Check that the spline is seated tight against the bottom of the slot. As a safety precaution, it might be a good idea to clamp the pieces if the splines are loose.

(16) The joint is sanded and finished, and the result is a strong and attractive joint. Using contrasting wood for the splines emphasizes the joint.   ☐

Mock Finger Joints, Cut by Hand

If the carcase you are working on is small and delicate, as in a small box, use splines made of veneer in kerfs made by a handsaw.

(1,2) Mark the 45° on the edge as a guideline to make sure the splines won't come through on the inside when you make the slots.

(3) Square the line across each side to mark off the depth of the sawcuts.

(4) Locate and mark the positions you want for the splines.

(5) Saw the spline slots with a handsaw. Choose a saw that will make a cut slightly thinner than the veneer to be inserted.

(6) Mark and **(7)** cut the spline pieces, leaving them a little oversized. The grain should run parallel to the bottom of the cut.

(8) Place the veneer on a piece of metal and hammer it so that it is thinner. Now the pieces will slide easily into the slots.

(9) Put glue in the sawcuts and **(10)** force it down inside the slots using your finger. Don't put the glue on the veneer splines. They will swell and you won't be able to get them in the slots.

11

12

(11) Slide the hammered veneer pieces into the sawcuts. Be sure you push the pieces all the way down. The veneer will absorb the moisture from the glue and will swell.

(12) Put a clamp across the joint to make sure that the joint will be tight. Clean off as much glue as possible before it hardens.

(13) When the glue dries, cut off the excess veneer and sand the surfaces.   □

13

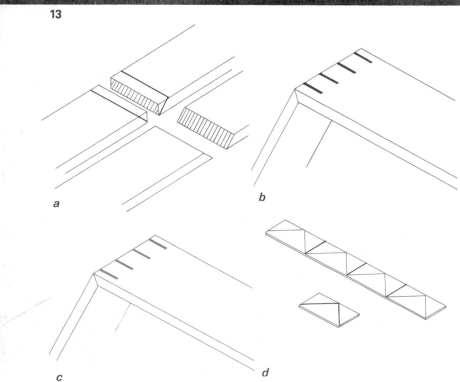

a

b

c

d

Router Table

It is very easy to make yourself a simple router table **(1)**. You will find it an indispensable tool for making joints, moldings and the like. Unless very heavy work is involved, it does just as good a job as a shaper. Also, you can feed the work from the top as well as the side. With a shaper, you can generally feed only from the side. The simplest table is made from a piece of ¼-in. Masonite or plywood. Drill a 1⅛-in. hole in the center. Remove the base from the router. Mark the position of the screws from the router base and drill holes into the plywood or Masonite. Fasten the router to the piece. You now have a very simple but very well-functioning router table.

A more stable router table is made in ¾-in. plywood. The best plywood for this is veneer-core. Mark the holes and drill them the same way as described for the simpler table. Here, though, you will have to rout out a circle **(2)** for the router to fit into on the underside of the plywood. This recess should be ½ in. deep, to leave only ¼ in. for the bit to go through.   □

1

2

1

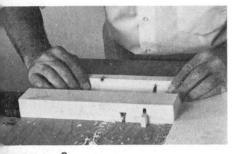

3

2

4

5

6

Mock Dovetails

(1) The jig for making a mock dovetail is exactly the same as the one for the mock finger joint (see p. 95), but the slots are cut in a router table using a dovetail bit, and the splines are made dovetail-shaped.

Set up a fence on the router table. The fence board has to be thinner than the bottom of the *V* in the jig. It is a good idea to rub the jig, fence and table top with paraffin or a candle so the jig will slide more easily.

Make a cut with the dado blade for the guide pin so it will fit snugly into subsequent dovetail cuts. Then locate where you want the dovetail cut in the piece. Mark the jig and set the fence for the cut. Because the dovetail cutter sits up high above the table so that it is able to come through the bottom of the *V* in the jig, you will have to make a cut in the bottom of the jig for the shaft of the cutter to pass through **(2)**.

(3) Make the dovetail cuts in the jig.

For the first cut in your final pieces, make a mark on the jig halfway between the dovetail cut and the guide pin. **(4)** Put the piece against the mark and make the first dovetail slot.

(5) Place the first slot over the guide pin, and continue down the piece until all the cuts are made **(6)**.

Tilt the table-saw blade to 80° and rip the splines. Then cut them to length **(7)**.

(8,9) Put glue in the slots and insert all the splines. When the glue dries, cut the tails flush with the surface using an offset dovetail saw, and plane and sand the pieces.

(10) Again, we have a very strong and decorative joint. The joint can be emphasized more by using a contrasting wood for the tails.   □

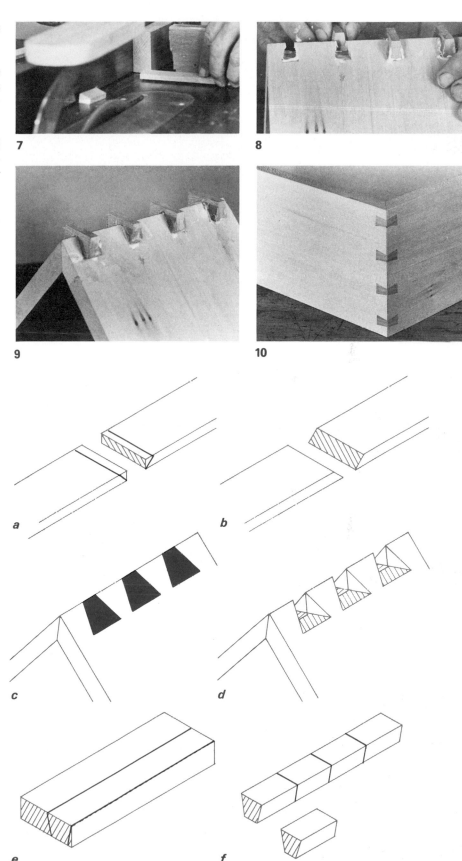

7

8

9

10

a

b

c

d

e

f

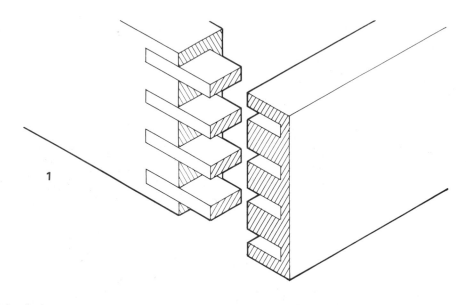

1

Half-Blind Multiple Splines

Multiple spline joints **(1)**, an outgrowth of router-made dovetail joints, are considerably easier to make than full-blind or half-blind dovetails. They are stronger than dovetails because of the greater amount of long-grain to long-grain glue surface. And, because they are cut by machine, they are made more accurately. The only machines required are a table saw and a router—the two most commonly used machines for making carcase joints. The router (with a straight bit) makes the slots the splines fit in, and the table saw (with a dado blade) makes the finger-like jig to guide the router.

The setup for making multiple spline joints takes very little time. The jigs can be used over and over again. The same jig is used for both the full-blind and half-blind versions of the joint.

Making the jig   To make the finger-like jig, you need to choose the collar you will use in the router. And the collar is determined by the size of the straight bit you will use. I use a ⁵⁄₁₆-in. bit, because ⁵⁄₁₆-in. thick splines are a good size. Once the collar is chosen, measure its outer diameter, in this case, ⁷⁄₁₆ in. **(2)**.

Then set the dado thickness so that it fits the diameter of the collar exactly. **(3)** Use thin pieces of metal or paper as shims for fine adjusting of the width of the dado cut. I use thin sheet aluminum.

When the correct width is set, **(4)** draw two lines extending from each side of the blade on the wooden insert in the table-saw top. These lines **(5)** will serve as guidelines when making the jig.

(6) Lay out the slots on a piece of ¼-in. or ⅜-in. plywood. The spacing isn't critical, but the distance between slots should be not more than twice the width of the slots. The idea is to get enough splines in the joint to get sufficient glue surface. The slot height isn't critical either, but should be at least ⅜ in. higher than the thickness of the wood to be joined. The exact length of the spline slots will be determined later by how the jig is placed on the wood being joined.

2

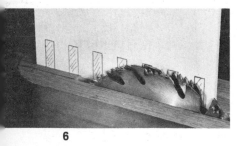

3

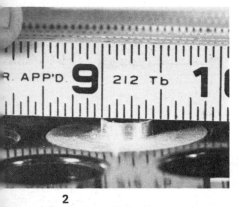

4

5

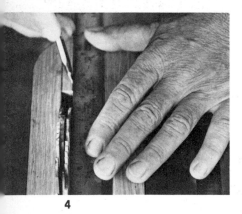

6

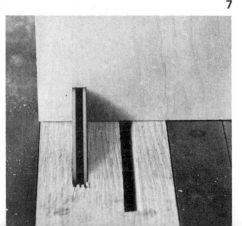

7

The jig has to be the same width as your actual pieces. Raise the dado head to the exact height of the slot, but to prevent the blade from tearing up the wood in the back of the jig, screw a piece of ¾-in. plywood to the miter gauge. Set the miter gauge to 90° and **(7)** make a cut.

(8) Use the two guidelines on the insert to line up the cuts.

(9) Cut all the slots across the piece of plywood, and the jig is finished.

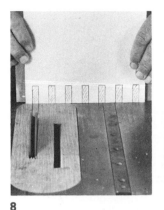

8   9   10

To determine where to place the jig on the board to be joined, you must first measure the space taken up by the router collar. **(10)** Place the base of the finger slot tightly against the collar. Measure the distance between the router bit and the base of the finger slot. In this case, the difference is ⅟₁₆ in.

(11) Set the bit to the right depth — approximately ¾ of the thickness of the wood. This determines how deep the mortises for the splines will be.

(12) To determine the length of the mortises, turn the board over and (in this case) draw a line ⅟₁₆ in. back from where you want the mortises.

(13) Now place the jig over the board and line up the bottom of the fingers exactly on the line.

(14) Clamp the jig onto the board and to the bench. Cut the mortises with the router, moving the router into each slot. The collar will guide the router into each mortise.

(15) Here the jig is still in place and all the mortises are cut.

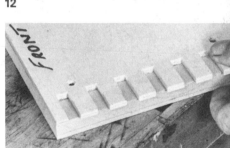

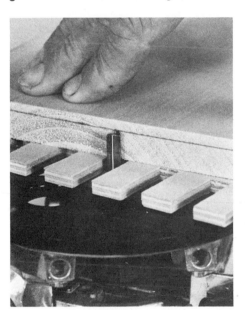

11   13

14   15

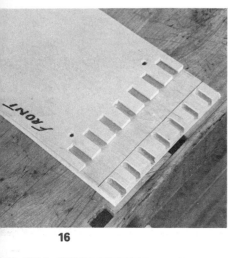

16

17

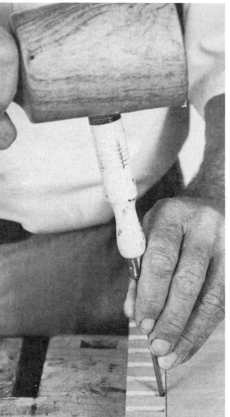

18

19

20

21

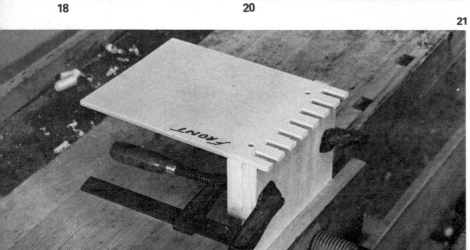

(16) The jig is removed to show the mortises.

(17) Using a marking gauge, scribe a line at the back of the mortises so that when you chisel the backs square, the mortises will all be the same length.

(18,19) Square off the bottoms of all the mortises with a chisel. Undercut slightly.

(20) To make the opposite part of the joint, scribe a line on the end of the board ¹⁄₁₆ in. deeper than the desired depth, or whatever the difference is between the collar and the router bit.

(21) Put the piece in the vise and clamp a scrap piece onto the back. Screw the jig onto that piece, making sure that the bottom of the mortise slots on the jig are right on the scribed line of the piece. Make sure that the orientation of the jig (the edge is marked "front") is correct. Now the pieces are ready to be routed, using exactly the same depth setting on the router bit as on the other piece.

(22) Allow the collar to guide the router into each finger.

The slots are cut. Here the are viewed both from the outside **(23)** and from above the jig **(24)**.

Again using the marking gauge, scribe the back of the slots so all the mortises will be the same depth when chiseled out **(25)**.

(26) The slots are squared off and **(27)** the backs of the slots are undercut slightly.

(28) Be sure the corners are clean so that the joint will go together all the way.

(29,30) Remember that the jig will have to be flipped over for the right and left sides of the cabinet so the slots will all match.

Making the splines The splines have to fit snugly into the slots. You can make them by running a piece of wood through the thickness planer until the board is the right thickness, and then ripping the pieces to the right width on the table saw. But I prefer to make the whole spline on the table saw. It is faster and easier, and I can use pieces of scrap wood, as long as they are thicker than the splines will be wide. If a piece of plywood fits into the mortise, it can be used for splines also — especially in the full-blind version where the splines will not be visible.

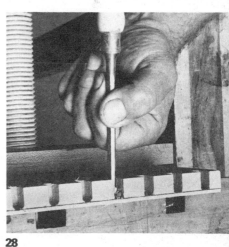

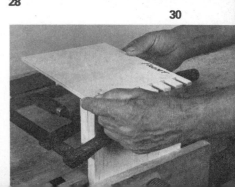

22

23

24

25

26

27

28

29

30

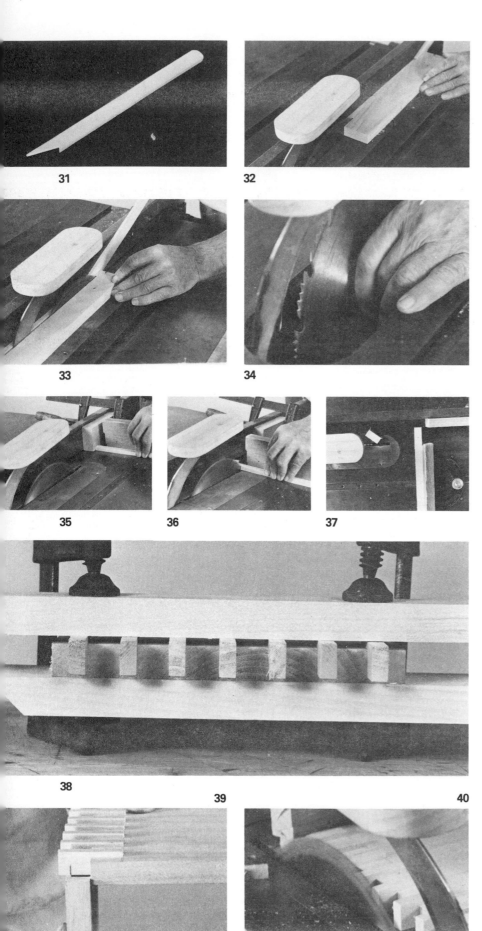

31

32

33

34

35

36

37

38

39

40

When cutting thin pieces, always use a push-stick at the end of the pass. The push-stick **(31)** should be thinner than the piece being cut. The back of the push-stick should be rounded and the edges softened, so that if the wood kicks back the push-stick won't cut your hand.

(32,33) Set the fence to the right width, (determined by the width of the mortises you have cut with the router bit) and rip all the splines.

(34) To cut the splines to length, use a hollow-ground blade (see pp. 21-23). A hollow-ground (also called a planer) blade makes a clean cut, and, because the teeth have no set, will not pick up the pieces and throw them at you, the way a blade with set to the teeth would. The splines should be about ¼ in. longer than needed. They'll be trimmed later to exact length.

To prevent the pieces from being trapped between the blade and the fence after they are cut (and getting thrown back at you), clamp a block to the fence and set the fence so that the distance from the block to the blade is the right length for the spline **(35)**. The block should be back at the beginning of the fence so that the splines will not get trapped.

(36,37) For each cut, slide the piece over to the block of wood to get the right length and then, using the miter gauge, move the piece up to the blade.

(38) When the splines are cut, glue and clamp them into the mortises of the piece cut first. Keep the splines a little higher than the finished size so that they can be clamped tightly into the mortises. When the glue dries, **(39)** mark and **(40)** cut the splines to the right length so that they fit the opposite part of the joint.

(41) Plane and sand the splines flush with the surface **(42)**, and the joint is ready to assemble **(43)**. To emphasize the joint, you could use wood of a different color for the splines.   ☐

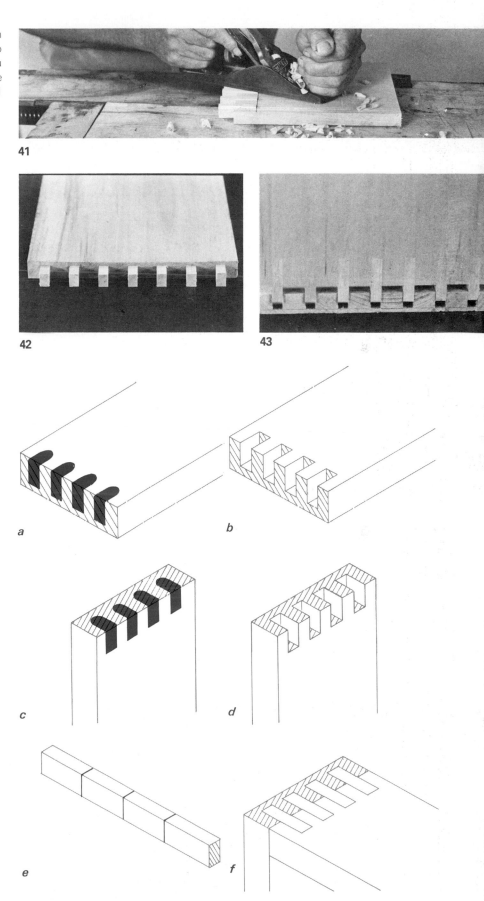

41

42

43

a

b

c

d

e

f

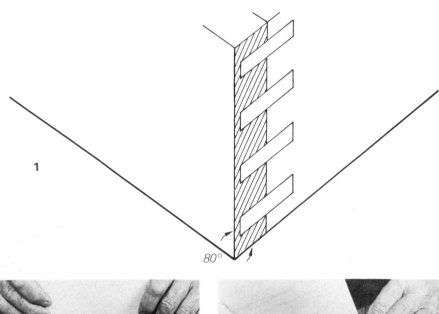

1

80°

Angled Half-Blind Multiple Splines

(1) The jig for routing this joint has to be made very carefully and accurately. The distance between the pins has to be exactly the same, because the jig won't be flipped over as for 90° half-blind splines, but will be turned 180°.

(2,3) To make this jig, the setup is the same as for finger joints, except that the dado blades are tilted to the angle of the multiple spline. So if the angle is 80°, the blade is tilted 80°.

The top and bottom edges of the tilting piece have to be cut to the desired angle, as in making angled dovetails (see pp. 78-79). **(4)** Clamp the jig on the tilting piece and then rout out the grooves.

(5,6,7,8) Now turn the jig 180° to make the opposite cuts. My right hand holds the second board to be routed and the pictures show the sequence of turning the jig in my left hand 180°.

2

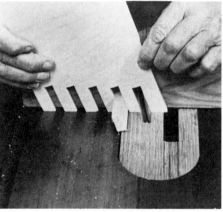

3

4

5

6

7

(9) Remove the piece screwed on, **(10)** clamp the jig securely to the second board and use the router.

Chisel the corners clean, then make the spline. **(11)** The joint is ready to be glued after all corners are cleaned.

(12) This joint can be very attractive and decorative with splines of a different color wood.   ☐

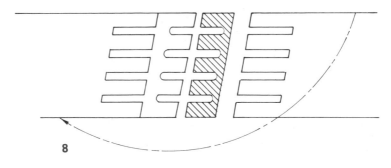

8

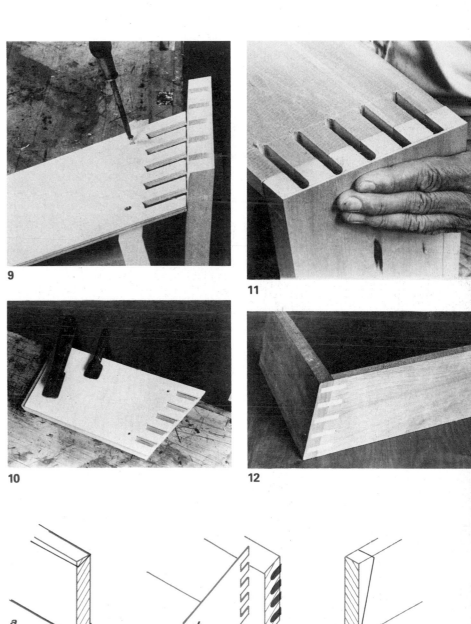

9

10

11

12

a b c

d e

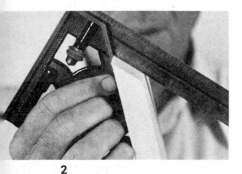
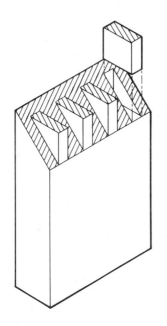

1

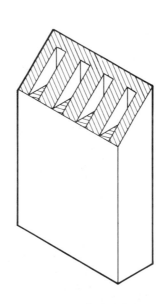

2

3

4

5

6

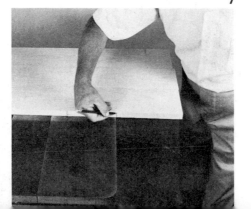

7

Full-Blind Multiple Splines

Making the full-blind multiple-spline joint **(1)** is like making the half-blind version, and the same jig can be used if the boards are the same width. The difference is that in the full-blind joint the edges are mitered so the splines are concealed inside the mitered corner.

When you set the saw to cut the miters, do not rely entirely on the saw's angle scale. Set the blade to 45° and then cut two pieces, each about 12 in. long, at the miter angle. **(2)** Don't bother checking the miter this way, with the 45° angle on an adjustable square. It is not accurate enough.

(3) Instead, put the two 12-in. pieces together, hold them tight and check the whole corner with a square. If the angle is wrong, adjust the tilt of the blade slightly and try again.

(4,5) Also check that the piece is square down the edge of the miter so that the pieces will meet in a clean corner the whole way down. If it isn't square, check your miter-gauge setting.

(6) Once the setting is correct, cut your final pieces.

If the board is too wide for you to use the miter gauge, you can make a fence to guide the board instead. Place the board on the table with the blade exactly in the position where it will cut the angle. Mark the end of the saw table onto the piece **(7)**.

(8) Square the mark across the underside of the board.

(9) Clamp a straight board right on the line.

(10) Then cut the miter.

(11) Mark 1⁄16 in. from the corner. This distance is determined by the thickness of the router collar and the size of the router bit (see p. 103).

(12) Square the line across. When the jig is clamped on, the bottom of the fingers must be right on the line the whole way across so the mortises will have the same depth. Here again, set the depth of the bit so that the mortise is about 3⁄4 the thickness of the board.

(13,14) Cut the mortises in the mitered pieces.

8

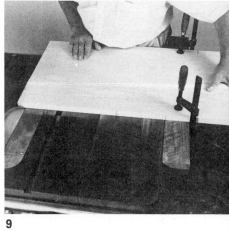
9

10

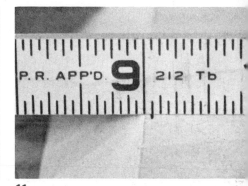
11

12

13

14

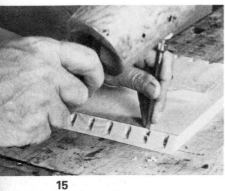

15

16

After the slots are cut, remove the jig, chisel the corners square **(15,16)** and be sure they are all clean **(17)**.

When making this joint, you will have to flip the jig over for the right and left sides so the slots will line up accurately. Place the two boards end to end **(18)**.

(19,20) Flip the finger jig over to ensure that the mortises will match when they are cut in the second board. Then clamp the jig on and repeat as before.

(21,22,23) When cutting the spline to the correct width, you must be very accurate.

17

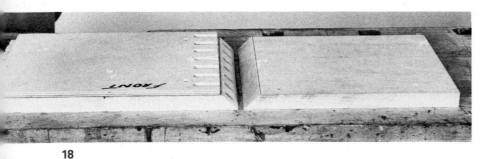

18

19

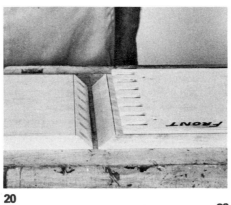

20

21

22

(24) The spline should be exactly flush with the inside piece so that it fills up the entire mortise.

When cutting splines to length, follow the same procedure as when cutting them for the half-blind joint (see pp. 105-106). But to be sure you end up with a perfectly square spline that will fill up the whole mortise, adjust the fence so that the stop block is exactly the spline width away from the blade **(25)**. If the splines are too big, the joint won't go together. If they are too small, you will have a problem lining up the corners. Keep the blade high so it doesn't catch the small pieces after they have been cut **(26,27)**.

(28,29,30) The joint is now ready to be glued up. But this time, glue the splines and both pieces together at the same time, because of the 45° angle. This can be a real disadvantage in a piece with many parts. Also, a lot of clamps are necessary in all directions to ensure a tight glue line, and to keep the pieces from sliding. If done carefully, the splines could be glued on one piece first, but be sure all excess glue is cleaned off. □

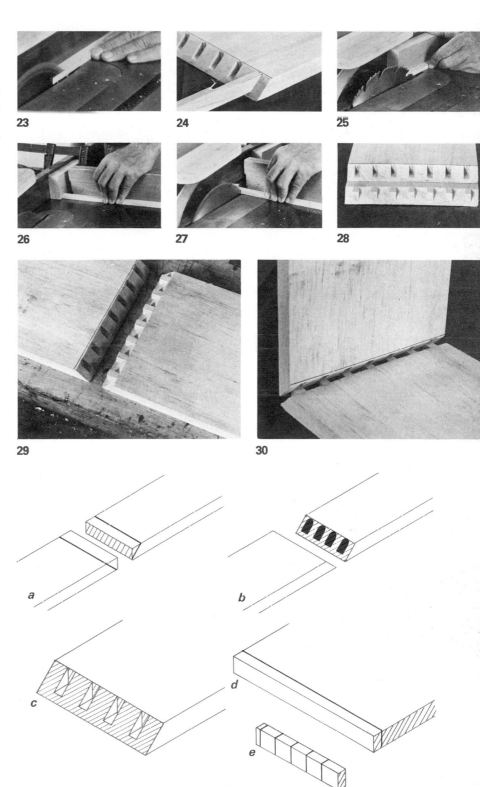

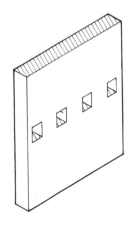

1

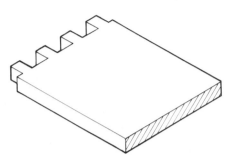

Multiple Tenons

Another strong and attractive carcase joint for mid-section structural elements is a series of small mortise and tenon joints **(1)**. This is an excellent joint in solid wood. The joint does not have to run all the way through the other piece, but running the tenons through and wedging them from the outside at assembly will add strength.

Using the marking gauge, mark the full thickness of the piece with the mortises onto the piece with the tenons (if the tenons are through tenons). This gives the depth or length of the tenons. Then lay out their width. If you are making them by hand, cut them out with a handsaw **(2)**.

(3) Remove the outside pieces with a handsaw. Don't undercut here—we want a tight joint, front and back.

(4) With a chisel, score a *V*-cut where you will be chopping out (as done in making dovetails—see p. 67).

(5) Chisel out the waste between the tenons. Here we do want to undercut in the back so the joint will go together all the way.

(6,7) An easier way to make the tenons is to cut them with a dado head. Mark the tenons and make the cuts. In the same saw cut you will make the cheek and remove the waste. One or two passes (depending on the spacing) should complete the tenon. If you are making a lot of joints at once, you can set up a finger-joint jig to make all the cuts the same and complete the joints faster (see p. 90). Remember to mark the width of the dado cut on the saw-table insert as a guideline.

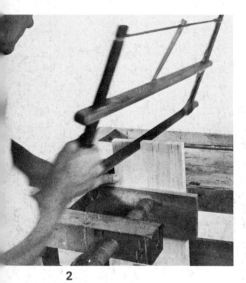

2

3

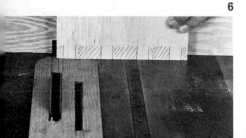

4

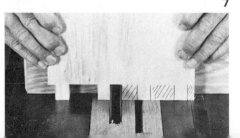

5

6

7

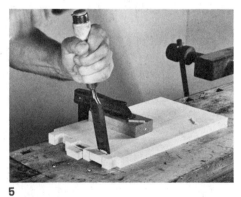

(8) When all the tenons are made, mark the full thickness of the tenoned board on the board the tenons are going into.

(9) Square the lines across.

(10) Mark the mortises from the tenons with a scriber. Be sure that the front side is flush **(11)**.

(12) Square the lines over to the other side. Scribe the tenons on this side the same way as you did on the other side.

(13) Draw diagonals from corner to corner to mark the center for the drill bit. Do this on both sides.

(14) Use either an auger bit or a spur bit to drill the holes. The bit should be slightly smaller than the finished mortise. Drill until the tip of the spur comes through on the other side, then flip the wood over and drill from the other side. This way the wood won't tear out in the back.

The holes are drilled. Now square off with a chisel **(15,16,17)**. Be sure to undercut the end grain in the holes. But the sides must be square to the surface to ensure good glue surface and a good fit.

8

9

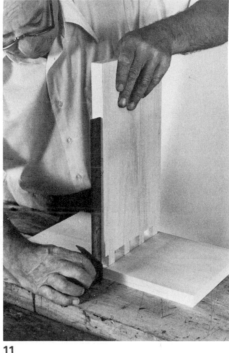

11

10

12

13

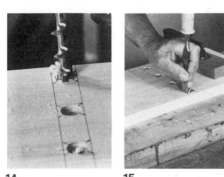

14

15

16

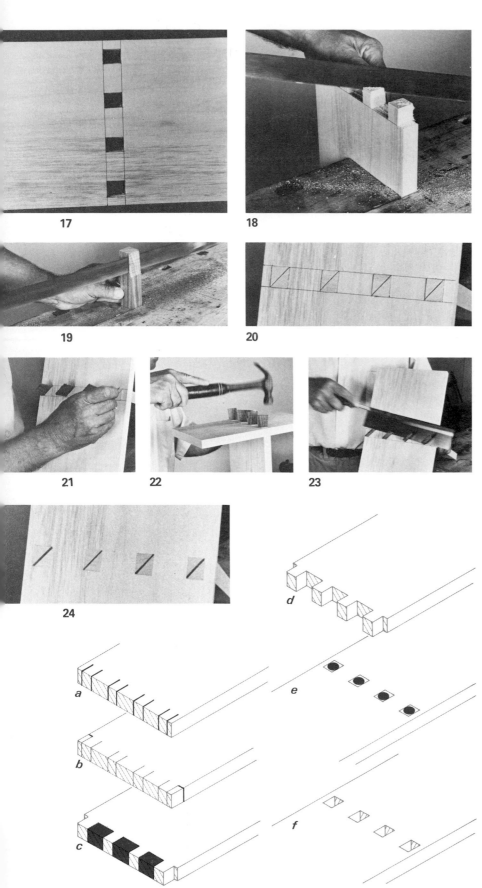

17

18

19

20

21

22

23

24

(18) Before gluing up make a sawcut from corner to corner in the tenons (for the wedges). This is done so that if for some strange reason the joint doesn't fit you can insert wedges to expand the joint so that it fits perfectly into the hole. When you glue and hammer the wedges in you will have a perfect fit. This is a good idea even if the tenons fit perfectly into the holes because it will add strength to the joint.

(19) The wedges can be made with a hand-saw or band saw.

(20,21,22) The wedges are glued and hammered into the diagonal cuts, then trimmed flush **(23)**.

(24) The joint is finished and sanded. It looks perfect—you will never know if it fit before the wedges were put in, and I am never going to tell you. ☐

Tongue and Groove
Chapter 7

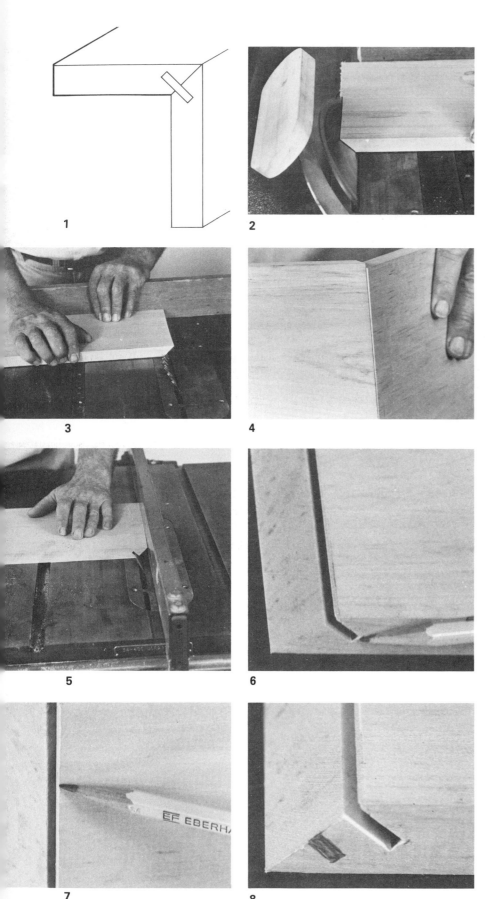

1

2

3

4

5

6

7

8

Diagonal Spline Miter

The spline miter **(1)** is a relatively strong joint, especially when used on veneer-core plywood — you will have 50% long-grain to long-grain glue surface. This is also a good joint for composition board, particle board, Novaply, etc. A spline miter is not a good choice for solid wood if strength is required of the joint. But it is all right for pieces such as small boxes.

Making a spline miter is very easy. First, cut a 45° miter in two scrap pieces to check the saw setting, and once you have the proper angle, **(2)** cut the miter in both pieces to be joined (as for full-blind multiple splines — see p. 110).

(3) Don't use the miter gauge for cutting the groove for the spline, because if the miter gauge is a fraction of an inch off square, the spline groove will not be parallel with the edge. Afterwards, when gluing the pieces together, the corners would not line up **(4)**. If you are using plywood, this could cause a real problem. When you sanded the corners flush you would go through to the veneer, and you would have an awful-looking corner. (But if you do go through the veneer, choose a felt-tipped marker the same color as the veneer and shade in the plywood to hide the mistake.)

However, the right way to cut the groove is to lower the blade and move the fence to the left side of the sawblade **(5)**. Raise the blade to the desired height, and cut the spline groove with the end of the board guiding off the fence. This method will keep the cut parallel with the edge and prevent the pieces from skewing as a result of a misaligned spline.

On a very narrow piece, use the miter gauge in combination with the fence to guide the piece through. To do this, push the end of the board tightly up against the fence. Move the miter gauge up to the side of the board and set it to whatever setting falls against the edge. This will prevent kickbacks in the cut.

Cut the groove for the spline as close as you can to the inside corner **(6)**, so you can get as wide a spline as possible. But do leave a small edge of wood towards the inside **(7)**. If a ¾-in. thick piece is used, I leave about a ¹⁄₁₆-in. edge, and I would make the thickness of the spline about ⅛ in.

(8) Here you can see how the spline gets narrower if it is moved closer to the outside corner.

If the spline miter is made in solid wood, the grain of the spline must follow that of the pieces being joined. **(9)** Here you can see how to cut splines on a table saw. If a lot of splines were needed, I would use a thickness planer first. **(10,11)** For safety, fasten a piece of wood to the fence with its lower edge higher than the piece you are cutting out so the piece doesn't get caught between the fence and the board.

(12) If the grain of the spline ran lengthwise down the spline, which would be across the grain of the pieces to be joined, the spline and the pieces would not move together, and the spline would be weak and could easily split.

If you use this joint in plywood, use a plywood piece for the spline, too. Make sure you have a piece that will fit snugly into the spline groove you make. Check the fit on scrap before you cut the spline groove.

(13) The spline in place.

(14) The joint assembled.   □

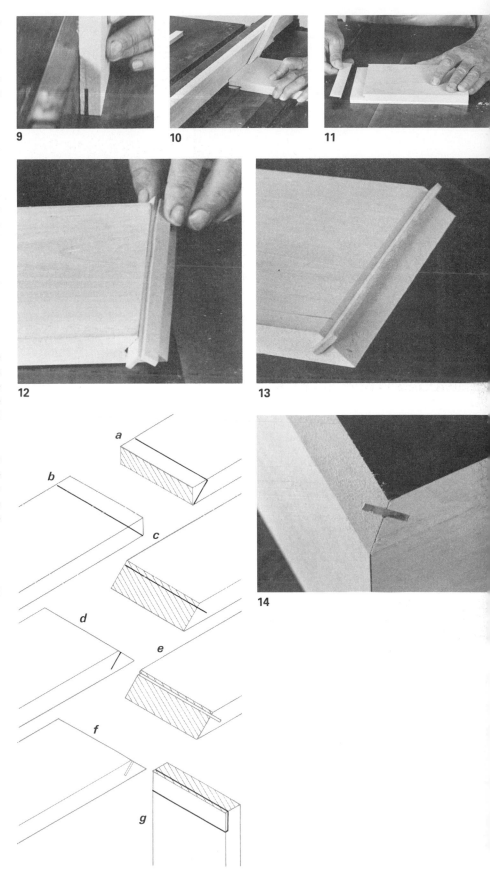

9

10

11

12

13

14

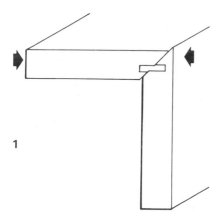

1

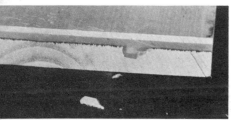

2

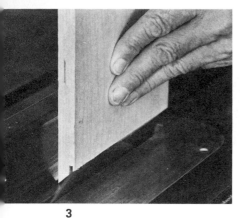

3

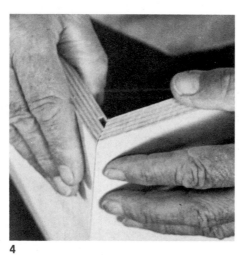

4

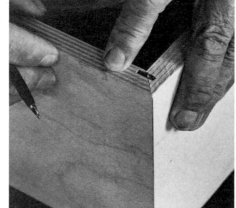

5

Parallel Spline Miter

The parallel spline miter **(1)** has several advantages over the diagonal spline miter (see p. 118), but it can be used only in plywood, and clamps are needed only in the direction parallel with the spline. The spline slots are minutely offset, about $\frac{1}{32}$ in., from one piece to the other. When clamped together, the spline will give a little, and the offset will pull the joint in tight.

The ease of clamping this joint is a real advantage. In a cabinet with many pieces, you can glue the inside and side members of the cabinet first, and when they dry, glue the top and bottom on. In some situations this might be much easier than trying to glue the whole thing together at once.

The joint is not for solid wood because the wood will chip off **(2)** and because the spline would be glued into only end grain in one of the pieces, which would result in a weak, unstable joint.

To make the parallel spline miter, you can cut the groove in the vertical piece with the wood running against the fence **(3)**. For safety, or with a wide piece, use the jig described in the section on splines for particle board (see p. 131). For very narrow pieces, use a tenoning jig (see p. 174).

(4,5) When you mark for the second cut, be sure to offset the spline slightly so that the pieces will pull in tight with clamps in only one direction.

(6) Cut the slot in the mating piece by running the edge up against the fence. With a narrow piece, use a miter gauge, setting it to the edge of the piece with the piece pressed tight to the fence.

(7) The grooves are finished.   □

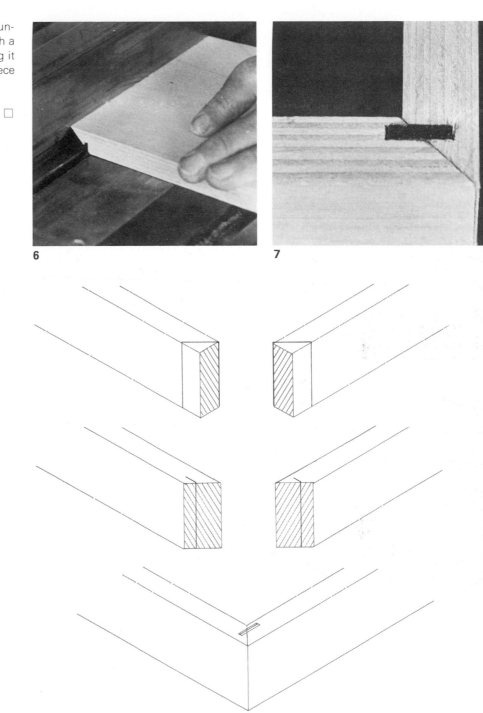

6

7

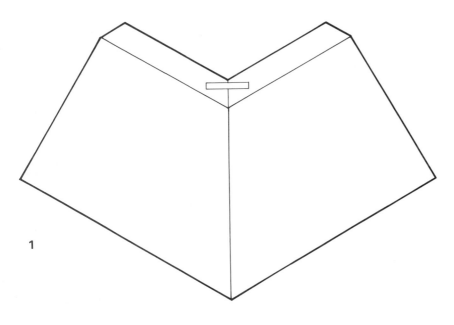

1

Compound Miters

To make a compound miter **(1)**, use the chart **(2)** to find the correct angle settings for the miter gauge and the sawblade. In this case I wanted to make a four-sided compound miter — where the sides are angled at 15° from the vertical and the corners come together in a miter joint. As the chart indicates, set the miter gauge to 75½° and the sawblade to a 43¼° tilt. Check the angles on two scrap pieces to make sure the pieces are square.

Sometimes you will have to adjust one of the angles (or even both angles) if the angle scales on either the saw or miter gauge are not accurate. To be sure of accuracy, check the angles by setting a *T*-bevel to a protractor and then transferring these angles to the miter gauge or sawblade. I always do a test set of joints **(3)**.

(4) Once the angles are correct, cut off the ends of the first board.

Compound Miters

Tilt	4-Sided Miter		6-Sided Miter		8-Sided Miter	
	Blade Tilt	Miter Gauge	Blade Tilt	Miter Gauge	Blade Tilt	Miter Gauge
5°	44¾°	85°	29¾°	87½°	22¼°	88°
10°	44¼°	80¼°	29½°	84½°	22°	86°
15°	43¼°	75½°	29°	81¾°	21½°	84°
20°	41¾°	71¼°	28¼°	79°	21°	82°
25°	40°	67°	27¼°	76½°	20¼°	80°
30°	37¾°	63½°	26°	74°	19½°	78¼°
35°	35¼°	60¼°	24½°	71¾°	18¼°	76¾°
40°	32½°	57¼°	22¾°	69¾°	17°	75°
45°	30°	54¾°	21°	67¾°	15¾°	73¾°
50°	27°	52½°	19°	66¼°	14¼°	72½°
55°	24°	50¾°	16¾°	64¾°	12½°	71¼°
60°	21°	49°	14½°	63½°	11°	70¼°

2

3

4

(5) For the second board, you will have to twist the miter gauge at the same angle, but measuring in the opposite direction. Another way to do this is to move the miter gauge to the groove on the right side of the sawblade, but use the miter gauge backwards **(6)**.

Raise the piece to 90° to the table and do not change the angle of the sawblade. The groove for the spline will then be at 90° to the compound angle. **(7)** With the piece clamped to the tenoning jig (see p. 174) and the edge of the miter down on the table, make the sawcut. **(8)** Then make a similar cut on the second board.

(9) The grooves are ready for the spline.

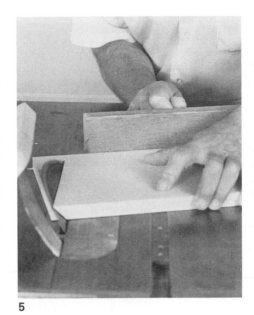

5

6

7

8

9

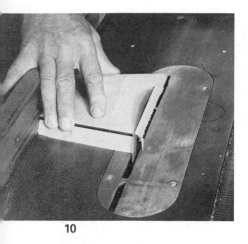

10

11

12

13

14

15

(10,11) Rip the two sides parallel at the same angle as the angle you want the joint to sit at. Since I want a 15° angle, I rip the edges to 15°.

(12) The result is a clean, tight, square joint.

(13,14) If you want the miter to be on the long-grain sides, first square off the boards, cutting the ends to the same bevel as the tilt (in this case 15°).

On tall pyramids, where long compound miters have to be cut, it would be dangerous to use the miter gauge **(15)**. Instead, make a jig out of plywood that will hold the work at the proper angle to the sawblade **(16)**. Use a piece of plywood long enough to give good support against the fence. Mark off the angle on the plywood and then draw a 90° line off the widest end of the angle. Bandsaw out the piece and you will have a jig that will house the piece to be mitered.

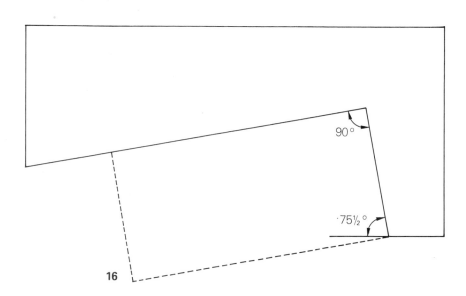

16

(17) In this case the board sits in the jig at 75½° — the same angle as the miter-gauge tilt would be. Draw a point on your board where you want the angle to begin (how wide you want the board to be, in effect) and move the fence the correct distance away from the sawblade. Make the cut, holding the piece securely in the jig. Save the cut-off piece.

(18) To make the second cut, reverse the jig and place the cut-off in the jig first, and then place the piece to be cut up tight against the cut-off. You can just hold the two together while you are running them through the saw, but this can be dangerous. I sometimes use masking tape on both sides to hold them together, but the safest way to keep them together is to glue blocks with paper underneath them over the two pieces. Use hot glue or some other quick-drying glue. (Use the same method as when gluing on corner blocks for clamping — see p. 127). If possible, it helps to have two people make the cut if you don't use the glue blocks.

17

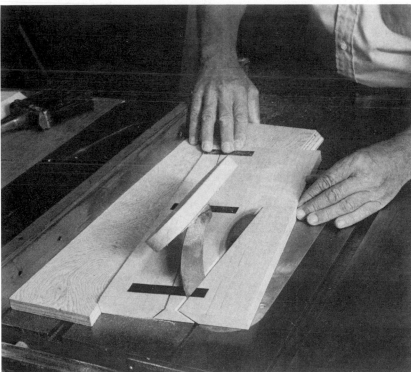

18

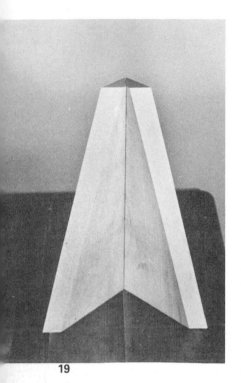

19

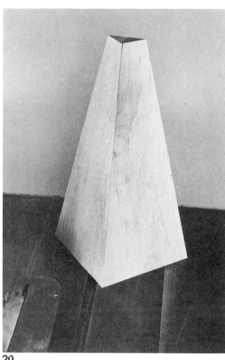

20

(19,20) The pieces should fit tight both inside and out. Since the glue surface is all long grain to long grain you don't really need a spline. But it is a good idea to use one so that the pieces will align properly when you are gluing them. Otherwise, they might slide all over the place as you try to get the clamps on.   □

Gluing Miter Joints

Gluing a 45° miter joint together is always a problem because of the difficulty in clamping the pieces. In a carcase, we have to clamp from all four sides simultaneously. In many cases we can't even see the corner because of the blocks and clamps involved.

I glue blocks cut to 45° with paper underneath them onto the pieces to be joined. This takes a little longer, but I have found that it is worth it. With the paper, the blocks can easily be removed by hitting them with a hammer. The paper will rip, and the blocks will come off easily without tearing up the surface of the wood.

(1) Locate where you want to place the blocks. They should be exactly across from each other on both sides.

Brush hot glue on the block. Use hot glue in a case like this because it sets fast and doesn't require clamps. Remember to glue the long-grain side. Then put the paper onto the block **(2)**. Don't use newspaper — use a heavier paper such as brown paper.

(3) Next put glue on the other side of the paper.

(4) Place the block in its location, and rub the block back and forth until it sticks.

(5) When all the blocks are glued on, let the glue dry before gluing up the joint.

(6) After gluing the joint, clamp the boards together.   □

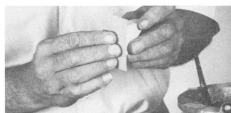

1

2

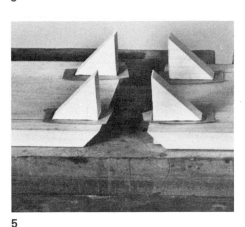

3

4

5

6

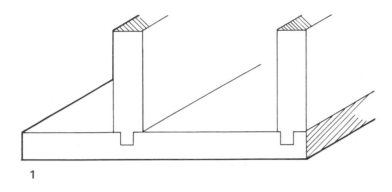

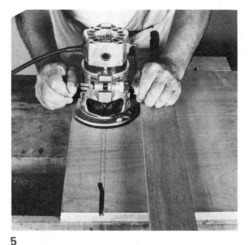

1

2

3

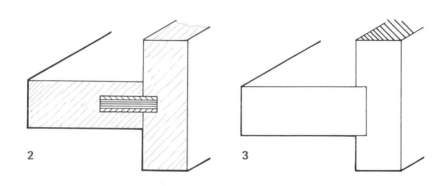

4

5

6

7

Tongue and Groove

A simple tongue and groove **(1)** can be used in any type of wood except composition board, but is best suited to plywood. If it is used on the end of a board, the tongue should be set off center so the outside shoulder is not too weak.

Fiberboard and particle board are both made out of waste material, so there is no grain strength. Since a tongue would break, a plywood spline **(2)** must instead be used with these materials. The spline should go into the carcase side about ⅓ the thickness of the side, and at least twice that amount into the perpendicular piece to add more strength.

I would never use a fully housed dado joint **(3)**. There is no shoulder to lock the wood and help maintain strength against sideways stresses. Also, if the wood is sanded after the joint is cut, the piece will become too loose. Even if you sand all the pieces before you cut the joint they will never all be exactly the same thickness, so your joint will be sloppy. Even plywood varies in thickness.

The easiest way to make the groove for the tongue-and-groove joint is on the table saw, if you don't mind showing the joint. If you are using plywood you will usually cover the edges with a facing, which would hide the joint. Use the dado blades set to the width of the groove and run the edge of the board against the fence if the piece is wide enough. Use a miter gauge to guide the board if it isn't wide enough.

If you don't want to show the joint, use a router for cutting out the groove. You can use a *T*-square as a guide for the router (see p. 132) and stop the joint before it goes through the front. Clamp the end of the *T*-square to the piece and let the base of the router slide along the extension of the square.

(4) If you start the router the wrong way, the router will tend to pull away from the tongue because of the direction in which the router bit is rotating.

(5) You can see how the cut pulled away from the line. If you want to use the side of the *T*-square as a guide, you must push the router away from you so the rotation of the bit pushes the router against the side of the *T*-square. If you use the other side of the square, you must pull the router toward you.

Once the groove is made, the easiest way to make the tongue is to use two sawblades or dado blades that are exactly the same diameter, and held apart by a spacer of wood or metal **(6)** that is the thickness of the tongue. With the spacer between the two blades, the blades will cut a tongue that will fit into the groove exactly. Once these spacers are made they can be used over and over again. (Of course, the shaper is the best tool for cutting tongues.)

(7) Measure the depth of the groove.

(8) Set the height of the sawblades so they are a fraction lower than the depth of the groove.

(9) Mark exactly where you want the tongue to be.

(10) Set the fence to the right distance, or use the tenoning jig (see p. 174). You could also fasten a high piece of plywood to the fence for stability, or use the jig for particle board in the section on splines (see p. 131).

(11) Make the double cut. Using the fence is quite safe because the cuts are very shallow.

(12) Set the height of the blade for cutting the shoulders. Use a blade that will cut across the grain.

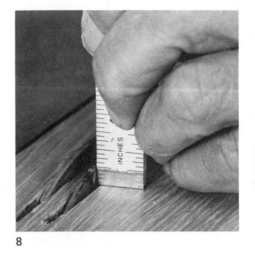

8

9

10

11

12

13

(13) Clamp or screw a piece of wood to the fence so the cutoff doesn't get caught.

(14) Mark and cut a section of the tongue in the front so the joint is concealed, and your joint is ready to be glued. Here, the saw-blades were too high when cutting the cheeks of the tongue, so the cuts are visible in the front. □

14

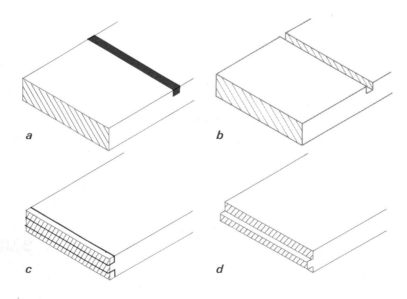

a

b

c

d

Jig for Cutting Grooves in Composition Board

Making a spline joint in composition board is like making a tongue-and-groove joint. Here, though, you make spline slots in both pieces, glue the spline into one piece, and then glue the two together as if they were joined with a tongue and groove. The groove in the perpendicular piece is done on the circular saw with a dado blade. The cut in the corresponding piece is made with the piece standing vertically against the fence. This cut should be twice as high as the first, to give the joint more strength. A special jig makes this cut an easier, safer operation.

The jig **(1)** will run over the fence to guide the pieces that will receive vertical saw cuts. This jig is particularly useful for tall pieces. You can clamp the pieces to the jig and move the jig down the fence to make the cut safely.

The jig is made of two pieces of plywood with a piece of solid wood sandwiched between. Dimensions for this jig are given in the drawing **(2)**, but you can easily change the dimensions to suit your particular needs.

Make and fit all the pieces. Be sure the solid piece between the plywood pieces is exactly the same thickness as the fence so there will be no play. The jig should be able to move freely through, so don't make it too snug. Clamp the jig together and check for fit and squareness before gluing it together.

(3) Be sure the jig is square to the table top of the saw.

(4) Set the dado blade to the depth of the groove you want and move the fence and jig to position the cut on the composition board **(5)**. Using the jig to make a tongue-and-groove or a tenon takes a little longer to set up but is considerably safer and more accurate than running the pieces through freehand.

(6) Here is the piece with the vertical spline slot with the spline inserted.   ☐

1

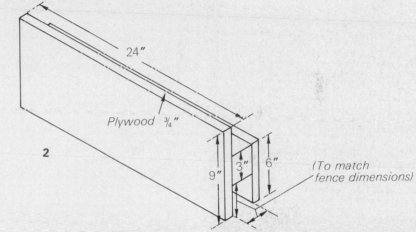

2

Plywood ¾"

24"

9"   3"   6"   *(To match fence dimensions)*

3

5

4

6

18"

3"

1

2⅞"   2⅞"

32"

Wood is ¾" thick.

3"

2

3

T-Square for Router

An easy way to guide the router for making straight grooves in a board is with a *T*-square made for the router. To make the square, take some ¾-in. stock about 3 in. wide that is exactly straight with parallel sides. Drill the holes for the screws, then glue and clamp the pieces together, checking to be sure they are exactly square. When dry, put in the screws.

The dimensions given in the drawing **(1)** are those I find most suitable for all-around work. For smaller work, make a smaller *T*-square. The distance to the bit mark depends on your router. Of course the same jig could be used for sliding dovetails (see p. 144).

(2) When the square is complete, use the router with the bit you will normally use for grooves to rout the ends of the square. The most common size I use is ¼ in. This locates the bit for your router in relation to the *T*-square arm.

(3) You can now use it for lining up the square in making cuts. ☐

Tongue and Rabbet

The tongue-and-rabbet joint **(1)**, really a tongue-and-dado joint, is very easy to make. It is not a very strong joint because end grain is glued to long grain. But it is good for small boxes, knickknack shelves and the backs of drawers. The proportions shown in the drawings should be strictly adhered to, because they are determined by factors of strength. The dado should be no deeper than one-quarter the thickness of the board. The thickness of the tongue should be about the same. If possible, don't make the joint flush. Move the dado in and the joint will have considerably more strength.

Before cutting the joint, sand the inside, especially the piece with the tongue. If you sand after the joint is cut, the fit might be too loose.

Choose a blade or dado setup ¼ to ⅕ the thickness of the wood. If the joint is going to be flush, set the fence to the exact thickness of the wood to be joined, so that the outside of the blade is flush with the outside of the edge **(2)**.

(3) Raise the height of the blade to ¼ the thickness of the wood.

(4) Holding the end of the wood up against the fence, cut the dado. If the board is very narrow, use a miter gauge or there will be kickback, but make sure the board presses snugly against the fence.

(5) Mark the thickness of the tongue on a scrap piece.

(6) Make the cut in the scrap, without changing the height of the blade. For safety, use a tenoning jig (see p. 174). Check to see if the piece fits. If so, make the cut in the good piece.

(7) Mark the piece to be cut.

Good   *Better*

1

2   3

4   5   6   7

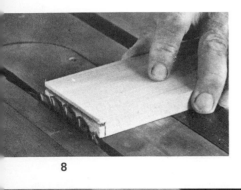

8

9

(8) Raise the blade to the right height.

(9) Push the end of the tongue against a piece of wood fastened to the fence, but raised above the small piece being cut, and make the final cut.

(10) The joint is ready to be glued up.   □

10

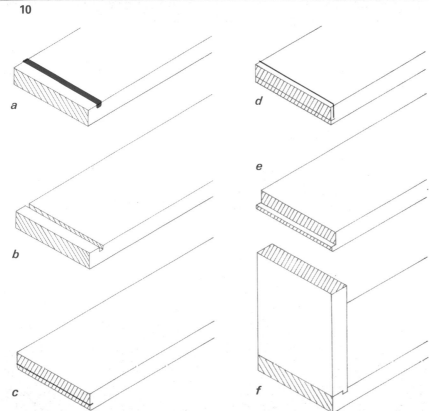

a

b

c

d

e

f

Half-Blind Tongue and Rabbet

(1) A half-blind tongue and rabbet (or dado) is similar to a half-blind dovetail but is not nearly so strong. It is particularly good for a drawer front. If used as such, the drawer stop must be put somewhere other than in the front because of the limited strength of the joint. If a router with a dovetail jig is available, I would definitely use it instead for joining a drawer front and sides.

When used in drawer construction, its most common use, the front is usually thicker than the sides. When making a half-blind tongue and rabbet (or a lock miter), always sand the sides before cutting the joint. Otherwise the joint will not fit as well.

The dado is cut exactly the same as in the through version (see p. 133), but not as far in from the edge because it's half blind. The pencil lines show how the joint should be laid out **(2,3)**.

(4) After the rabbet is cut, mark the tongue.

(5) Then measure the thickness of the sawcut required and **(6)** make your dado blade that thickness.

(7) Raise the dado blade to the exact thickness of the board that has the rabbet in it.

(8) Make the cut with the dado blade. Using a tenoning jig (see p. 174) to hold the wood is the safest way to make the cut. Try a scrap piece first.

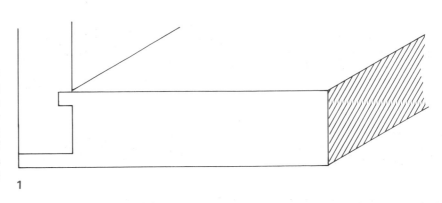
1

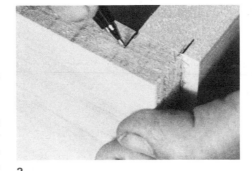
2

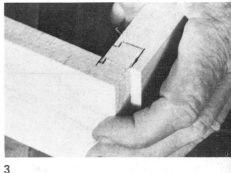
3

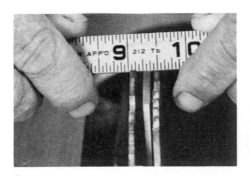
4

5

6

7

8

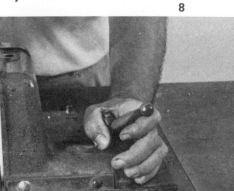

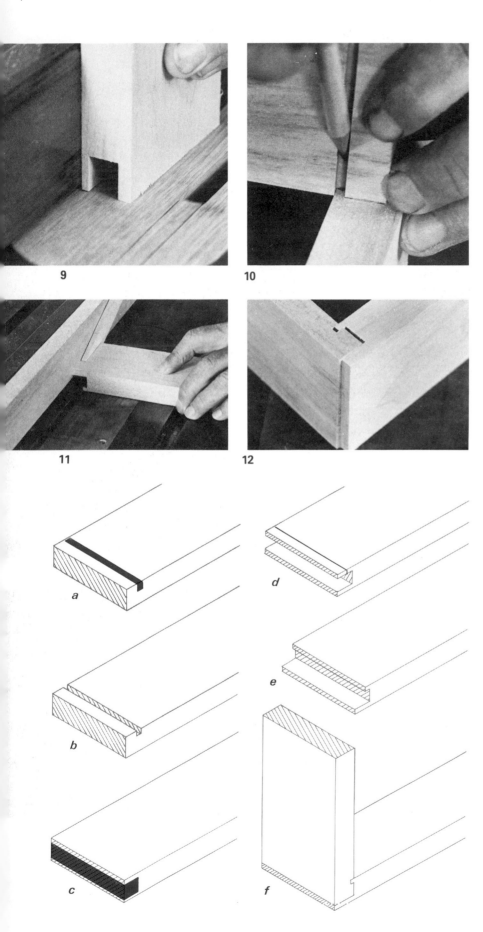

9

10

11

12

(9) If I am using a soft wood and the blades are sharp, I run the board against the fence. This is much faster, but I would not advise doing so until you are 100% sure of yourself, as it is much more dangerous, especially if you don't know what you're doing.

Then mark **(10)** and **(11)** cut the tongue to length.

(12) The joint is finished, and ready to be glued together.   □

a

b

c

d

e

f

Lock Miter

The lock miter **(1)** can be used in either solid wood or plywood, but it is stronger in plywood. Its advantages are that it is hidden from the outside and that it requires clamping in only one direction because of its built-in locking action. It is a strong joint, but not as strong as the full-blind multiple spline (see p. 110).

(2) Although the joint looks complicated, if you follow through the steps in the drawing you will find it easier than you think. I would suggest having several scrap pieces the same thickness on hand. Use them to check the accuracy of the fit at each step. This joint will be considerably easier if you have made the tongue-and-rabbet and the half-blind tongue-and-rabbet joints first. In the lock miter, though, you will be working with pieces of the same thickness, and you will have a few more steps to complete.

Great care must be taken when marking the wood and setting the machine cuts. First make sure the fence is set for the exact thickness of the wood, with the outside of the blade flush with the outside edge of the wood **(3)**.

(4) Raise the blade so it makes a rabbet ¼ the thickness of the wood and **(5)** make the first cut, using a push-stick or a miter gauge on the fence side. Check to see that the cut is at the right distance in.

Mark for the second cut. This is taken from the dado width and should be about half the thickness of the wood. After setting the dado blade, raise it up to the full thickness of the piece **(6)**.

(7) Use a tenoning jig (see p. 174) to help make the cut.

(8) Then check it for depth against the other piece.

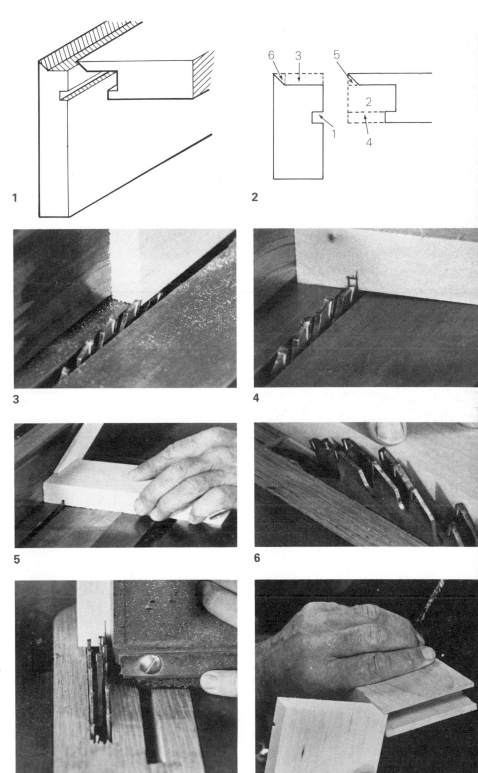

1

2

3

4

5

6

7

8

9

10

11

12

13

14

(9,10) Mark for the third cut.

(11) Attach a board to the fence higher than the cut you are making so the piece you are cutting off won't get trapped between the blade and the fence, and make the cut.

You can use a dado blade, or use a single blade and simply break off the excess **(12)**.

(13) Mark for the fourth cut. Again, fasten a piece of wood to the fence so the cut-off doesn't get trapped.

(14) Make the fourth cut.

(15) Lower the blade, move the fence over to the other side of the blade and tilt the blade 45°. Attach a thick piece of wood to the fence so it is higher than the blade but low enough to slide the tongue against. Make the fifth cut.

(16) Reset the fence and make the sixth cut, the final bevel.

(17) The joint is now finished.   □

15

16

17

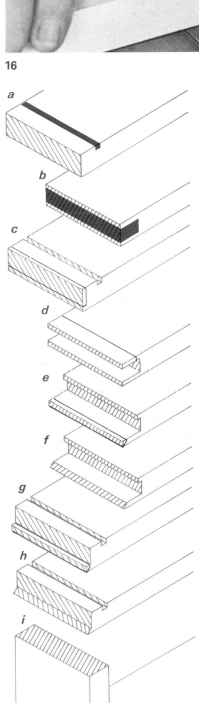

a

b

c

d

e

f

g

h

i

Sliding Dovetails, by Hand

A sliding dovetail **(1)** is very important in carcase construction. It can be made by hand or by machine. It works in any type of wood. It is easy to make, especially after you have goofed it up ten or twelve times until you get the hang of it. If I have only one or a few to make, or if the piece is very wide, I prefer to make them by hand. This way it is easier to fit, and the joint slides together more easily because it is tapered.

(2) Locate and mark the full thickness of the piece on the board it is to be joined to.

(3) Square the lines across, and **(4)** mark the end of the groove (to keep the joint hidden in the front).

(5) If ¾-in. lumber is used, mark ⅛ in. in from one of the lines at the back.

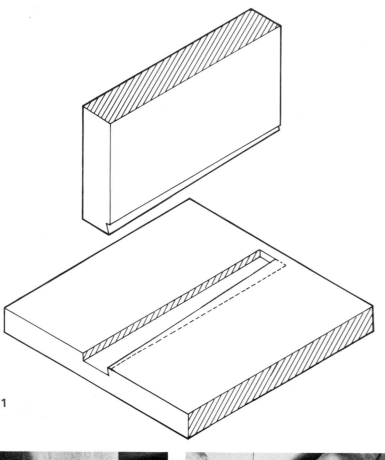

1

2

3

4

5

(6) At the front, on the same line, make a mark in ¼ in. Connect the points to form a new line **(7)** that will represent an overall taper of ⅛ in.

(8) Scribe the lines

(9) Score the lines with a chisel.

(10,11) Make a V-cut down both lines. This is important as it will provide a groove for the dovetail saw to slide in.

6

8

7

9

10

11

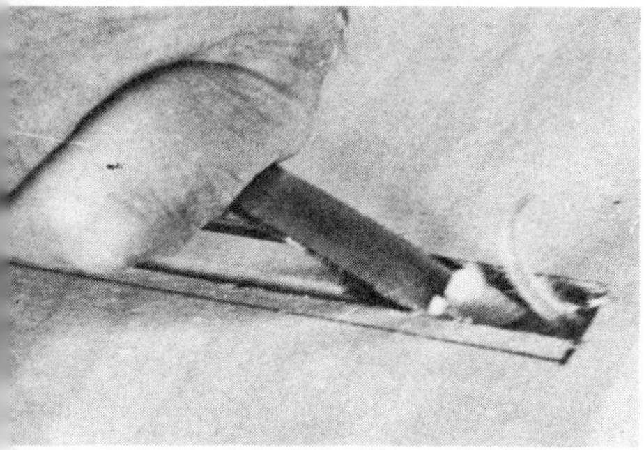

12

13

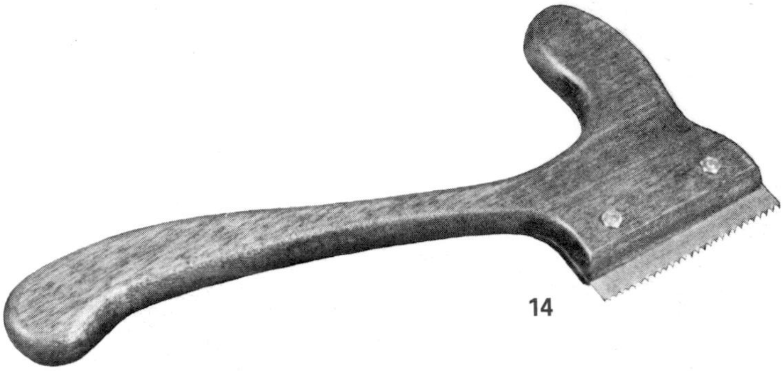

14

(12,13) Chisel out the front for the stop.

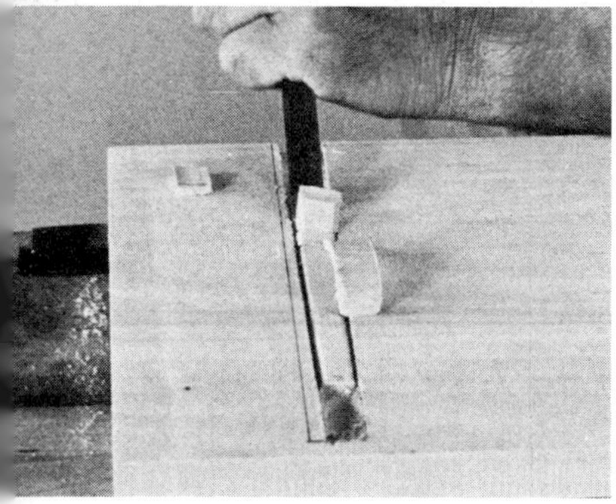

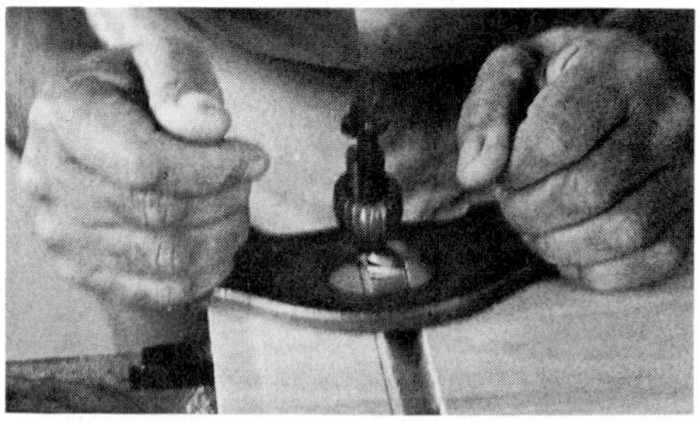

Saw the lines with the sliding dovetail saw **(14)**, which is designed for cuts like this (see p. 146).

(15) On the line that is square, keep the sawcut square or undercut just a little. The depth of the cut should be approximately ⅓ the thickness of the board, but should never exceed ½ in., no matter what the thickness is. The same is true of the tapered cut.

(16) For the tapered cut, tilt the saw to approximately 80°.

With both cuts finished **(17)**, rough-clean the groove with a chisel **(18)**.

Use the router plane **(19)** for the final cleaning of the groove so that it will have a consistent depth **(20)**.

(21) The groove is now ready to be fitted for the sliding dovetail.

(22) Mark the length of the tail with the blade in the router plane that cleaned out the groove but move it just a little back so the tail will be a little shy of the depth, to be sure the dovetail will fit tightly.

15

16

17

18

19

21

20

22

A dovetail plane **(23)** is like a rabbet plane, but the bottom is tilted about 80°. Because a dovetail is usually made on the end of a board, a knife in the front of the plane blade cuts the fibers so the blade doesn't tear up the board.

(24,25) Set the fence of the dovetail plane at the mark made with the router plane.

(26) Plane the piece to form the angled edge, and keep trying the tail in the groove to see if it fits **(27)**. When you have the piece in the groove, try and move both the back and the front up and down. If one end is looser than the other, plane off the tight end and test again. When the joint fits, you should be able to push it in by hand except for the last two or three inches (depending of course on the width.) Because the joint is tapered, it will fit tightly when the piece is hammered up to the end. So I put glue on only the last two or three inches in the front.

(28,29,30) Before gluing up, remove the piece in the front so the joint will be flush.

The finished joint, seen from the back **(31)**, after it has been glued and hammered home, and from the front **(32)**.   □

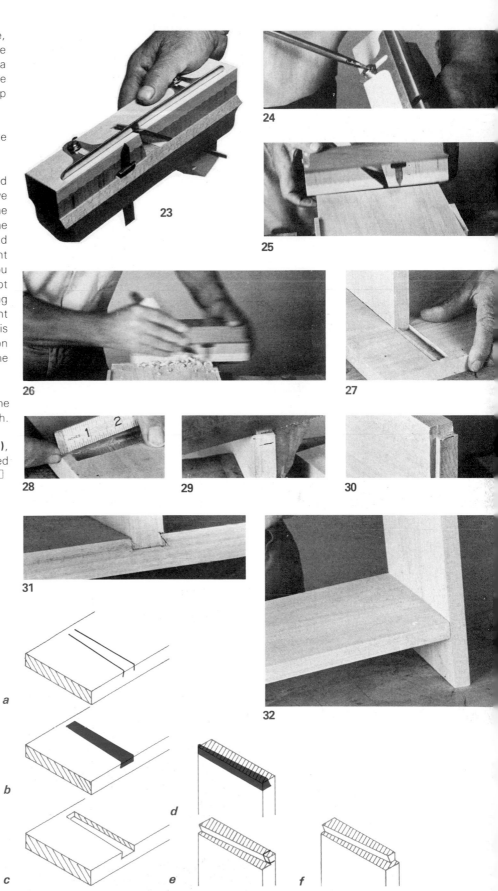

1

2

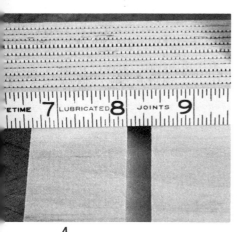

3

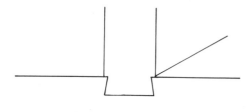

4

5

6

Straight Sliding Dovetails, by Machine

(1) To make a sliding dovetail by machine, use a router with a dovetail bit, the same way as when making a tongue and groove (see p. 128).

Either clamp a board across the plywood router table to serve as a fence, or **(2,3)** use a board or the same *T*-square used in a tongue and groove (see p. 132) to guide the router. With this method, both sides of the groove will of course be angled. In very dense woods, it is easier to run a straight bit first to remove most of the stock.

To locate the right size for the dovetail, measure the width of the groove at the top **(4)**, and then mark the piece to be cut **(5)**.

Using the router table, set the depth of the fence to make the right size sliding dovetail. On a scrap piece of wood the same thickness as your actual pieces, run one side.

(6) For the second cut, reset the fence over the router, keeping the same side of the board up against the fence. This way, if there is a difference in the thickness of the wood to be cut, the dovetail will still be straight. Great care must be taken when setting up to make the dovetail because the groove is not tapered, and therefore it has to be exactly right or it won't work.

(7) Here again, notch out the front of the joint if you want it hidden.

(8) The joint should fit so that you can hit it in with your hands except for the last couple of inches. Then use a mallet.   ☐

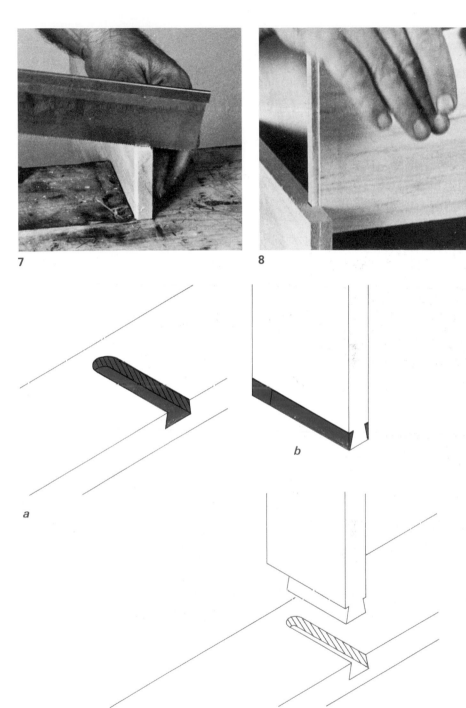

7

8

a

b

c

1

Making a Sliding Dovetail Saw

To make a sliding dovetail saw **(1)**, you will need a piece of hardwood (maple, beech or fruitwood) 1 in. by 5½ in. by 13 in., and two flathead $\frac{3}{16}$ by 1-in. bolts with *T*-nuts. The blade can be an old band-saw or bowsaw blade. It should have ten points to the inch, although eight will do. I use a ripsaw blade, which I find cuts better and faster than a crosscut. The slots allow the blade to be set to the desired depth. ☐

Jig to Rout Tapered Sliding Dovetails

(1) You can make a jig out of ¼-in. plywood that will enable you to make a tapered sliding dovetail slot with a router instead of by hand.

(2) Mark the full thickness of the board that is to house the tail onto the jig. In this case the board is ⅞ in. thick, and I want the depth to be ⁵⁄₁₆ in.

(3) Square the lines across. The collar in this case is ⅜ in. and the dovetail bit at its widest is ½ in., a difference of ⅛ in., which makes the bottom edge of the bit stick out ¹⁄₁₆ in. beyond the collar.

(4) Mark the line that will stay square ¹⁄₁₆ in. in from the squared lines. Square this line across.

(5) Make a mark ¹⁄₁₆ in. from the back of the other line.

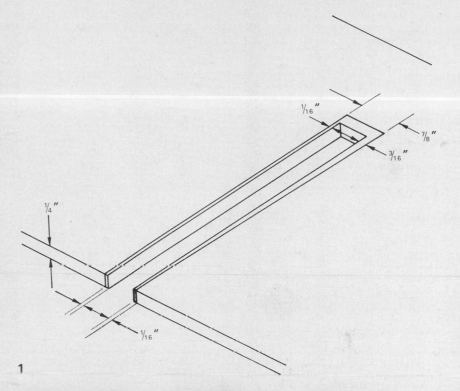

1

2

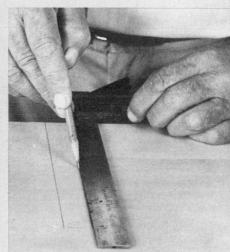

3

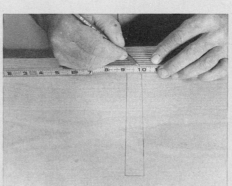

4

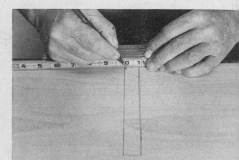

5

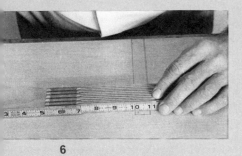

6

7

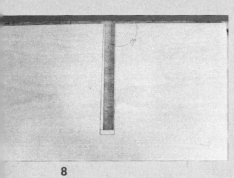

8

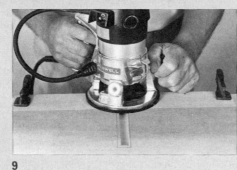

9

(6) Mark ³⁄₁₆ in. in at the front end of the same line.

(7) Draw a line to connect the two points and shorten the length of the cut if you don't want the joint to show through in the front. Then cut out the center section.

(8) Here is the jig, ready to be used. It can be used over and over again for many, many cuts.

(9) With the jig clamped down to the piece that will be routed, let the router collar follow the edges of the jig.

When you make the corresponding piece, do exactly the same as when making a straight sliding dovetail by machine (see p. 144). But since this piece is tapered, I would make the final passes by hand with a dovetail plane. ☐

Corner Tongue and Groove

The corner tongue and groove **(1)** is a good joint in solid wood or plywood. In plywood, tho grain of tho oornor piooo muot run lengthwise along the edging. In solid wood, the grain must run in the same direction as the grain of the sides so the corner and sides expand and contract equally.

The grooves in the plywood are cut like a simple tongue and groove (see p. 128). The tongues in the corner pieces are a little more difficult.

(2) When marking the position of the tongue, especially if you are using plywood, place two pieces of veneer under the plywood so the solid wood sticks out a veneer thickness beyond the plywood. If it were not, you might sand through the plywood when sanding the joint.

First cut the cheeks of the two tongues. Then cutting the outside two shoulders is easy. Remember to screw a piece of wood on the fence for safety **(3)**.

(4) The first inside shoulder cut is made exactly like the outside shoulders. Of course, you will need to raise the blade to the correct height.

For the next cut, make a jig as shown **(5)**. This jig screws onto the fence. The center is cut out to clear the blade, and the bottom piece is dimensioned so the shoulder of the tongue will run over it, making an otherwise dangerous cut very safe.

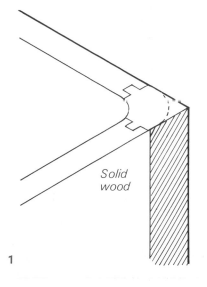

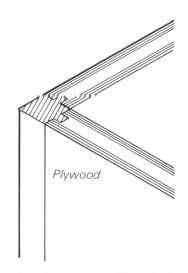

Solid wood   *Plywood*

1

2

3

4

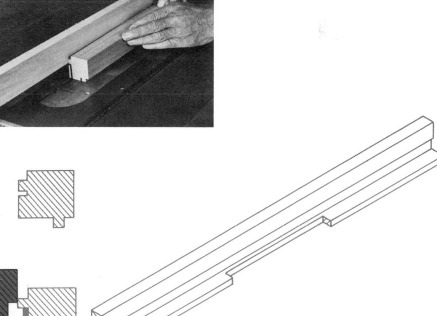

5   *Blade*

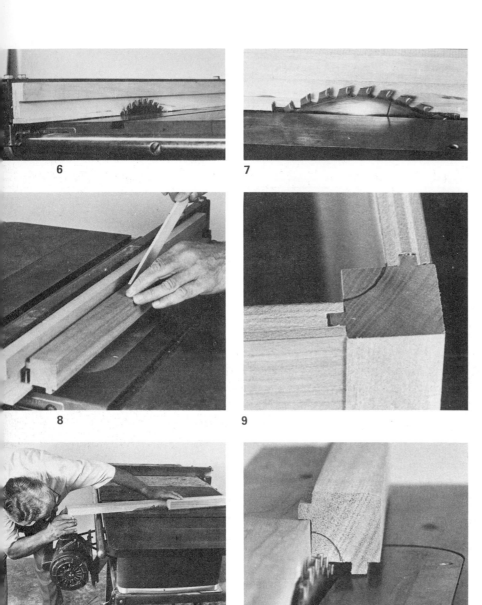

6

7

8

9

10

11

(6,7,8) The joints have now been cut. In this case I want to round the inside corner **(9)**. The easiest way to cut the curve on the inside is to make a cove cut on the table saw before gluing up the joint.

A cove cut is made by running the piece against an angled fence made of wood and chiseled out to make room for the blade. Since the front of the blade and the back of the blade will cut the pieces at different positions the result will be a curved cut. This is something that is very hard to visualize, but once you see it done you will believe it. Clamp a piece of wood across the saw table. The angle depends on the size of the cove. I place the piece to be cut up against the angled piece, eye it out from the back, and move the angled piece until the circumference of the blade fits the curve of the cove I want **(10)**.

In picture **(11)**, the fence is at the wrong angle. In **(12)**, the angle is correct. Note also that the fence fits exactly under the tongue so the piece rides securely on the fence.

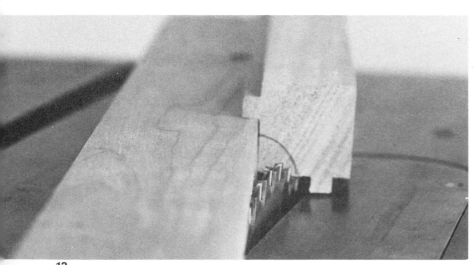

12

(13,14,15) Don't try to take the whole cut in one pass. Start slowly, and keep raising the blade so that it cuts about ⅛ in. with each pass. Leave a tiny bit of wood to allow for sanding.

(16) After sanding, glue the pieces together. Leave the outside corners square so you have something to set the clamp on when you are gluing up.

After the glue has dried, cut the corners off, then hand-plane and sand them round **(17,18)**.

If you want to hide the joint there is a little problem, especially if using plywood. The end of the corner block is end grain, which is not the best thing to glue veneer or a facing to. Before gluing any facing or veneer on, you have to glue-size the end grain. A glue size is a very thin layer of hot glue. Here it is applied to the end grain to seal the pores. If the glue has the right consistency (see p. 94), I would use about 1 part glue to 5 parts water. When the glue size dries, it will prevent the glue used to apply the facing or veneer from soaking in, and you will get a fairly good bond. ☐

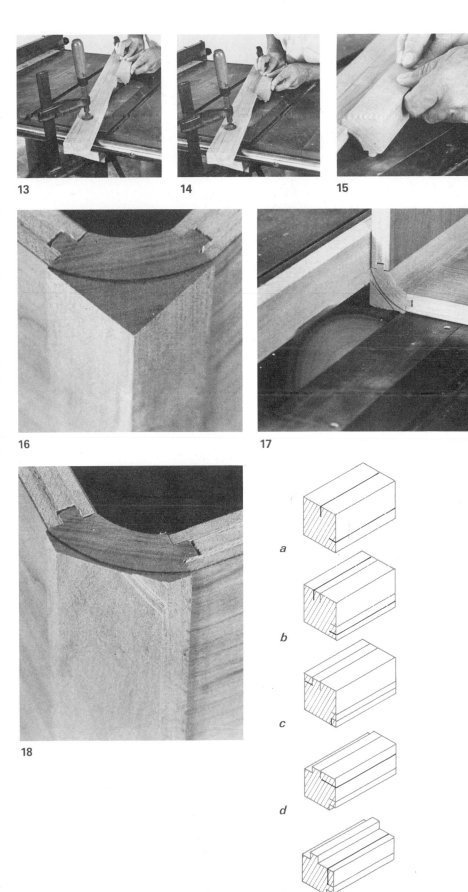

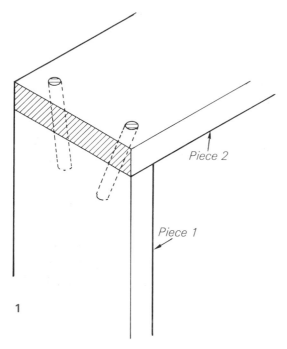

Piece 2

Piece 1

1

Doweled Butt Joint

I generally don't use a butt joint with dowels **(1)** but it is a stronger and more attractive joint than one with "steel dowels" (nails). If I do use the doweled butt joint I angle the dowels to add needed strength to the joint. In piece 1 the dowels are surrounded by long-grain to long-grain glue surface, a good glue joint. But in piece 2, the dowel is in mostly against end grain. So the dowels are set in at opposite angles, to act something like a dovetail. Even if the glue didn't hold, the angled dowels would hold the pieces together.

When you make the joint, first square all the ends that will be joined. Use hot glue to keep the pieces together when drilling the holes for the dowels.

(2) You can drill the holes using a brace and auger bit. Steady the auger using the weight of your body to apply some pressure. Use your head — literally. To control the depth of the hole, put a piece of masking tape on the bit at the depth you want and stop drilling when the tape reaches the surface **(3)**.

(4) You can also use an ordinary electric drill. For depth, use the tape, or even better, make a wooden guide. Drill a hole through a block of wood big enough for the bit to fit through. Cut the block to the right length. It should fit between the chuck of the drill and the depth you want to go into the wood. The bit (not including the point) should stick out the same amount as the depth you want the hole to be. This same method can be used for auger bits or any kind of drill. I prefer the block to other stops that you can buy. These are usually made out of steel and fasten to the bit or drill. When the full depth is reached, the steel stop will usually mark or scratch the surface of the wood. Using a wooden block is much better. When the block hits the surface it will stop rotating, especially if the bit or drill fits loosely into the hole in the wooden stop.

2

3

4

5

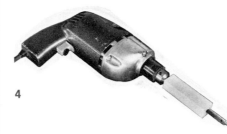

6

When the holes are drilled, cut off some sections of dowel longer than the finished length. Chamfer or soften the edges of the dowel so they will slide in easily without marring the edges of the holes. You can buy a dowel sharpener **(5)** to chamfer the edges. I prefer to use sandpaper **(6)**.

(7) Put the glue in the hole, not on the dowel. Don't overdo the glue—don't spatter it all over. The dowel will push the glue into the hole as it is hammered down **(8)**. If glue is put on the dowel, all the glue will be scraped off at the edge of the hole. Hardly any will get into the hole. When the glue dries, cut the dowels off flush with an offset dovetail saw.   □

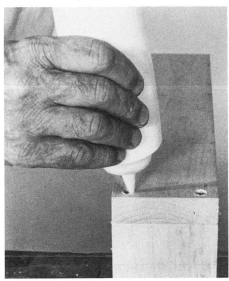

7

8

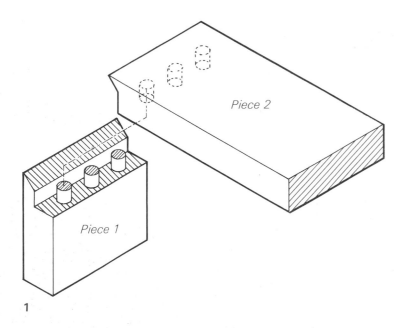

1

Hidden Doweled Miter

The hidden doweled miter **(1)** is used where structure is not critical—in small boxes, cabinets, spice racks and the like—where we don't want the joint to be exposed. This joint is as strong as a half-blind tongue and rabbet (see p. 135). The hidden doweled miter is an easy joint to make. It aligns itself correctly for gluing because of the dowels. This joint works in either solid wood or plywood, but is best suited to plywood.

(2) Make the cuts and the miters first, the same way as for lock miters (see p. 137).

(3) Now drill the holes in piece 1.

You can then use dowel centers **(4)** to transfer the position of the holes in one piece to the corresponding holes in the other piece. I don't use dowel centers. It is an extra thing to buy and you usually need quite a few of each size. I use wire brads instead. They work just as fast and as well, and are considerably cheaper. And you don't need any special sizes for each hole.

(5) Hammer the brads three-quarters down into the center of where the holes will be in piece 1. I use 1-in. wire brads, #16.

4

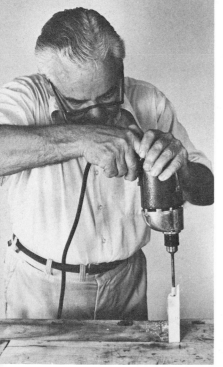

3

5

2

(6) Then bite off the heads, leaving about ³⁄₁₆ in. sticking up.

(7) Put piece 2 in place and hit it with your fist or with a mallet to mark the holes in the corresponding piece **(8)**.

The two pieces are marked. Remove the brads and drill the holes **(9)**, using the brad marks as centers for the dowel holes.

(10) Bits come in many shapes and sizes. You can use a brace and auger bit (third from left), or an electric hand drill with a spur or spade bit (three rightmost bits). I prefer the spade bit in an electric drill.

When drilling the holes in piece 2, be sure to mark the depth on the bit **(11)** so the bit doesn't come through the outside. Use masking tape if you want to make the mark more visible.

(12) Chamfer the edges of the dowels and glue the dowels into piece 1.

(13) After the holes are drilled in piece 2, measure their depth.

(14) Mark the dowels that are already glued in piece 1. Make them shorter than the holes in the opposite piece; the amount shorter depends on the thickness of the wood used. In a ¾-in. thick piece, I would make them ¹⁄₁₆ in. shorter.

6

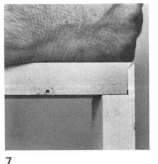

7

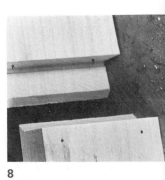

8

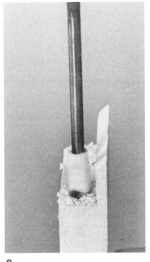

9

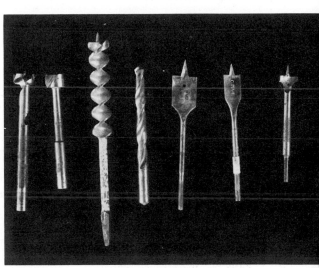

10

11

12

13

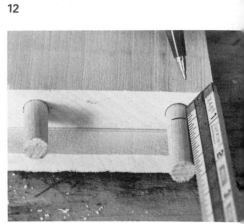

14

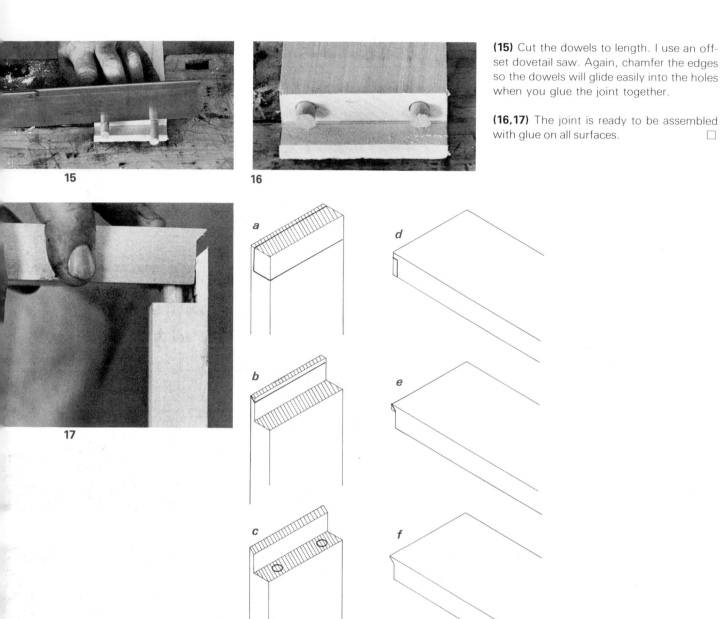

15

16

17

(15) Cut the dowels to length. I use an off-set dovetail saw. Again, chamfer the edges so the dowels will glide easily into the holes when you glue the joint together.

(16,17) The joint is ready to be assembled with glue on all surfaces.   ☐

a

b

c

d

e

f

Doweling for Frame Joints

I would never use a dowel joint to construct a frame that needed to be very strong, but for simple frames, a dowel joint might be enough **(1)**.

Although I usually use brads instead of dowel centers to position dowel holes precisely (see p. 154), here I'll demonstrate the use of dowel centers while making a frame dowel joint. Dowel centers **(2)** are available in different sizes.

Begin making the joint by drilling holes in one of the boards, and insert the dowel center **(3)**.

(4) I usually begin in the end-grain piece. For me it is easier to line up and mark the pieces this way. But you could start with the other piece.

(5) The opposite piece is marked. If you line up the pieces correctly the dowel center will mark the exact location of a hole that will correspond with the first hole. Now drill the other holes and glue the dowels into the first piece. Be sure to hammer the dowels all the way to the bottom. Measure the depth of the hole in the second piece, and cut the dowels to length, leaving them ⅛ in. shorter than the depth of the hole. This way, the excess glue has somewhere to go.

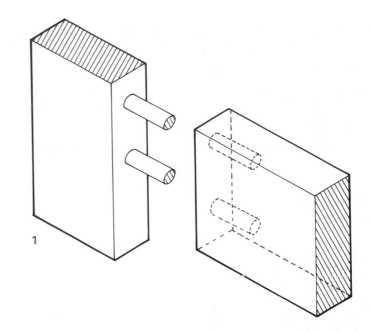

1

2

3

4

5

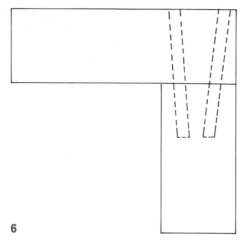

6

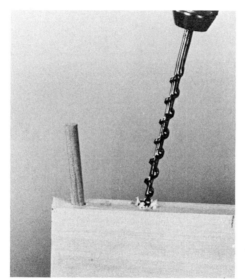

7

8

If I use a dowel joint, I try to make it as strong as possible, so I usually run the joint through. I don't mind the ends of the dowel showing. **(6)** This is the dowel joint I prefer. I always drill the holes at opposite angles, with the wider portion at the top, to make a "dovetail" effect. In the lower piece the dowel is surrounded by long grain, so there is a lot of strength. But in the upper piece, this is not the case. By angling the dowels, the upper piece is held securely, and a reasonably strong joint results.

(7) Before drilling the holes, glue the frame pieces together using hot glue. Drill the holes after the glue has dried enough so that the pieces won't move. Make the holes at about an 80° angle, using either a hand or machine drill. A wooden dowel jig like the one on p. 170 but made at an angle may help the beginner to drill the holes accurately.

When gluing in the dowels, it is very important to put the glue in the hole. Usually, I also put a spot of glue around the bottom edge of the dowel, which helps the dowel to slide in, and the glue pushes up as the dowel is hammered down **(8)**.   □

Mortise and Tenon
Chapter 8

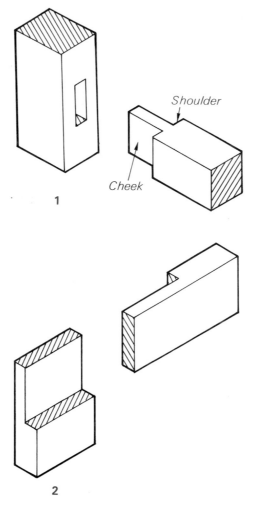

Shoulder

Cheek

1

2

Frame Joinery

The mortise and tenon is one of the oldest and most essential joints in woodworking. An Egyptian sarcophagus now in the British Museum was framed with mortise-and-tenon joints at least 5,000 years ago. During the Middle Ages, the development of the mortise permitted the framing of chests. Elaborate variations of paneling led finally to a distinction between the crafts of carpentry and cabinetmaking. In house construction, the use of the mortise and tenon has just about disappeared. We no longer have the skill or the patience, nor can we afford the time, to use mortise-and-tenon joints to frame houses. But still we find esthetic and practical satisfaction in making a well-constructed piece of furniture.

Many different types of mortise-and-tenon joints and both simple and complicated variations will be described. The joints will be made by different techniques. This is not meant to show that one technique is the best way to make each joint. All of the techniques can be interchanged from joint to joint. For example, a slip joint will be made by hand—sawn with a bowsaw. The same technique could be used for sawing any mortise and tenon. And the slip joint could be made on the circular saw. My intention is to show you as many ways as possible to make all the joints so that you can suit the techniques to your own equipment and personal choice.

A mortise-and-tenon joint should be designed and made so that it has the maximum long-grain to long-grain glue surface. The strength of the mortise-and-tenon joint depends entirely on the interplay between the cheek and shoulder of the tenon, which is the projecting part of the joint **(1)**.

If two crossed boards are glued together, they can be twisted apart relatively easily, because it's only the glue that holds them together and prevents them from twisting. The strength of the joint can be greatly increased by taking a small amount off each of the touching surfaces, thus creating shoulders to prevent twisting. The full use of such a design is called the half-lap joint **(2)**. It is the easiest frame joint to make, and is so called because usually half the amount of wood is removed from each piece. Each piece has one cheek and one shoulder. The strength is greatly increased because of the stopping action of the shoulders. The cheek is the glue surface that holds the joint together, and the shoulder, which should be tight up against the edge of the joining piece, makes it impossible for the piece to wiggle loose.

Now double the surface area of the glue by making a slip joint **(3)** — a form of mortise and tenon — and we have an extremely strong joint that is easy to make and requires minimum tools. The disadvantage of the slip joint is that not only do we have to clamp the tenon shoulder tightly against the mortise, (as in all mortise-and-tenon assembly), but we must use a second clamp to make sure the cheeks are glued to the mortise sides.

We get around these drawbacks by changing the slip to a haunched mortise **(4)** where only part of the joint is exposed, or to a mitered haunched mortise **(5)** where the tenon is completely hidden.

When designing a mortise-and-tenon joint, one should aim for the maximum glue surface. A tenon of about one-third the thickness of the stock is usually the best choice. If the tenon is thicker, the mortise sides become too thin; if the tenon is thinner, it becomes too weak. (But sometimes in table construction, where the leg is much thicker than the aprons, the aprons may have tenons half or more the apron thickness.)

Four shoulders **(6)** should never be used unless absolutely necessary. The joint becomes more difficult to fit because all four shoulders must be precisely located in the same plane. Also, glue surface is lost. On the other hand, if the design calls for carving and material will be removed around the joint, four shoulders ensure that the joint will not be revealed.

(7) If the design calls for round corners, it is advisable to glue a block on, or to have the mortise stock wider. These provisions prevent problems with the end grain, which will break and crumble, especially if carved.

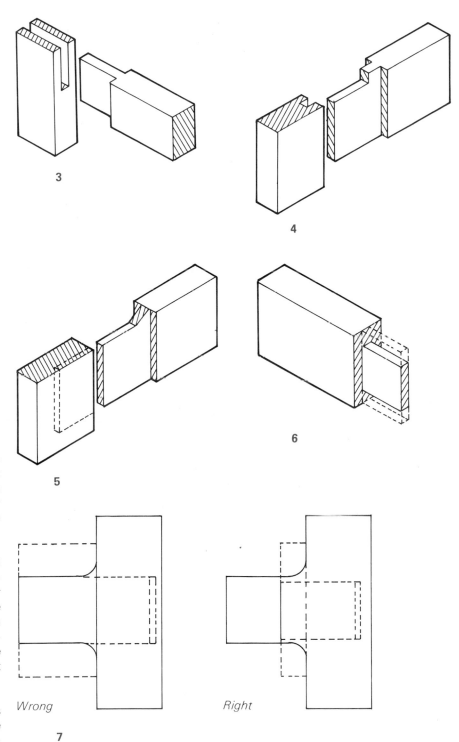

3

4

5

6

Wrong

Right

7

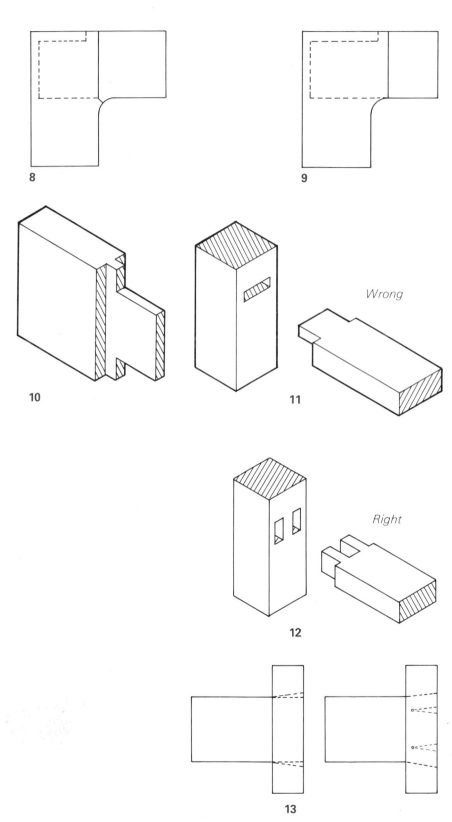

8

9

10

11

Wrong

12

Right

13

There are two different ways to make a round corner in a frame. One **(8)** is used if the inside corner is going to be carved or shaped for a molding, and the other **(9)** is fine if the edge will be left straight, because then you don't have to worry about carving into the joint. (But in fine cabinetmaking, carved or not, I would not use this joint.)

(10) When a tenon is very wide, haunches should be put in at either end. A wide tenon is more difficult to glue because it requires extra clamps for gluing the cheeks. But the haunches are necessary to keep the wood from twisting.

(11) When the stock is very narrow, the temptation is to run the tenon across the grain. But this should never be done because then the cheeks glue into end grain, which is not a glue surface. The way to join the pieces is to use double (or triple) tenons **(12)**, running the mortises in the direction of the long grain to provide good glue surface.

(13) Wedges can be used to strengthen the joint. When the tenon is cut to receive the wedge, be sure to drill a small hole at the base of each sawcut to prevent splitting. When hammering in wedges in a through tenon, be sure to hammer evenly on each wedge so as not to force one half or the other too far, which could result in splitting. If the tenon is to be hidden and wedged, use this method.

(14) If a mortise and tenon is to be disassembled, a loose wedge is used. The wedge could be replaced with a wedged dowel for the same effect. If the piece that receives the wedge is too thin, the two shoulders could be placed on the top and bottom instead of the sides.

In a chair, the back is usually one or two inches narrower than the front. This is done more for appearance than for any other reason. This requires the sides to angle into the back. Usually the angle is made in the tenon **(15)**, because it is easier than angling the mortise. Of course there is a limit to how much the tenon can be angled, but as long as some long grain reaches the full length of the tenon, it is safe. Notice that the tenon in the side apron going into the back leg is longer than the tenon in the back apron. The reason is that the joint in the side apron is more important.

(16) A variation of the slip joint is used where a third or fourth leg is necessary, as in a sofa. This is also used where a table apron is joined to the legs if the table apron is bricklaid round or oval, as in a Hepplewhite table.

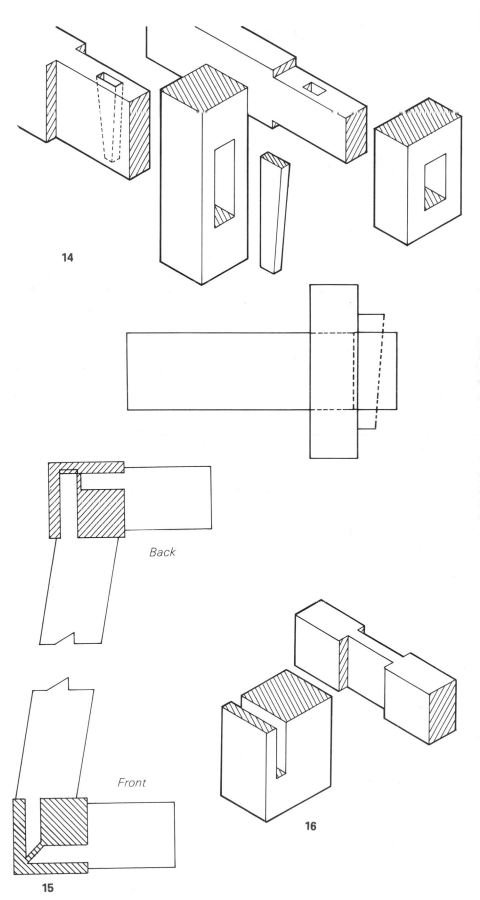

14

Back

Front

15

16

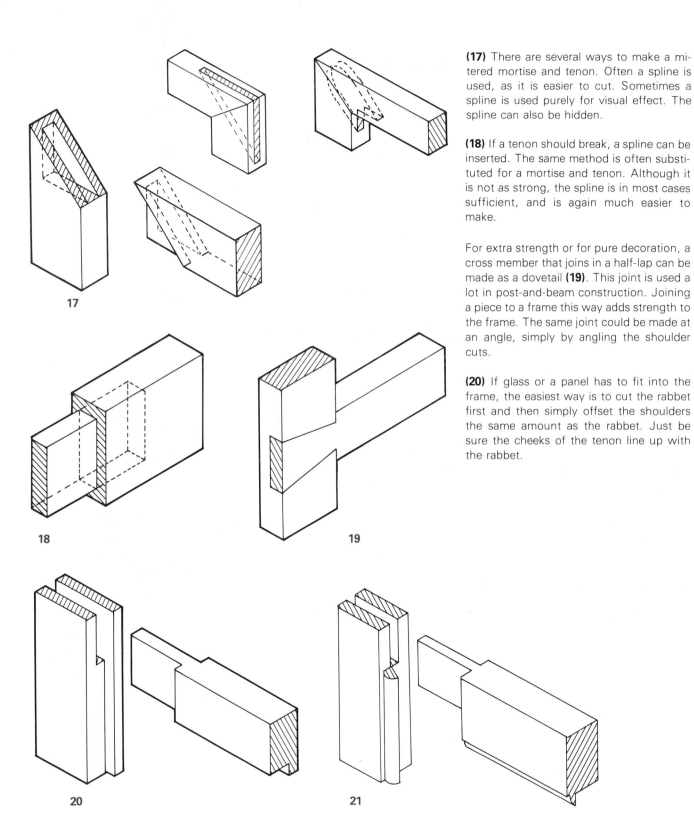

17

18

19

20

21

(17) There are several ways to make a mitered mortise and tenon. Often a spline is used, as it is easier to cut. Sometimes a spline is used purely for visual effect. The spline can also be hidden.

(18) If a tenon should break, a spline can be inserted. The same method is often substituted for a mortise and tenon. Although it is not as strong, the spline is in most cases sufficient, and is again much easier to make.

For extra strength or for pure decoration, a cross member that joins in a half-lap can be made as a dovetail **(19)**. This joint is used a lot in post-and-beam construction. Joining a piece to a frame this way adds strength to the frame. The same joint could be made at an angle, simply by angling the shoulder cuts.

(20) If glass or a panel has to fit into the frame, the easiest way is to cut the rabbet first and then simply offset the shoulders the same amount as the rabbet. Just be sure the cheeks of the tenon line up with the rabbet.

The next joints are drawn as slip joints because they are easier to explain this way, but they could be made as haunched joints instead. If both pieces to be joined have a molding and will receive a panel or a piece of glass, the easiest way to get the profiles to meet is to cut them the full length of the pieces first, **(21)** cut the profiles to 45°, and then remove the rest of the profile at the joint. When I was young, we used two cutters that met perfectly, one for each side of the molding profile **(22)**, and called them male and female cutters. But today we can no longer use the sexist terms male and female, so I refer to them as person-to-person cutters. If I have to build many frames of the same pattern, I have a set of person-to-person cutters made and cut the moldings on a shaper — that would be the easiest way. You could use a router, too. With a router, first make the joint on the tenon piece, then rout the profile (in this case the negative profile) in the shoulder.

(23) If a panel is to be inserted into the frame inside a groove, try to make the tenon the same width as the groove, or at least a little bigger. Also remember to deduct the depth of the groove on the inside width of the tenon **(24)**. Be sure to remember one thing — if a solid wood panel has to be inserted into the groove, never glue the panel in. If you do glue it in, it will definitely split.

There are many other variations of the mortise and tenon, but virtually all depend on the cheek and shoulder action for their strength. Similarly, the technique used in making these joints is basically the same. □

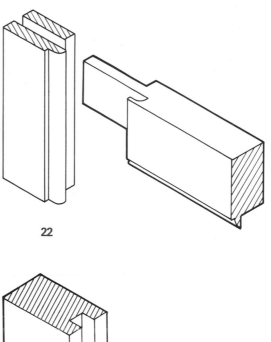

22

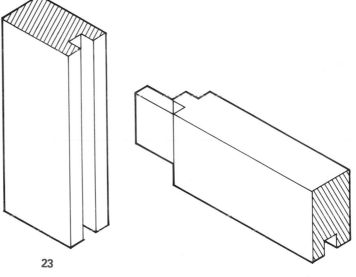

23

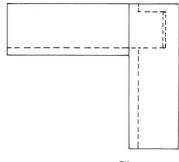

24

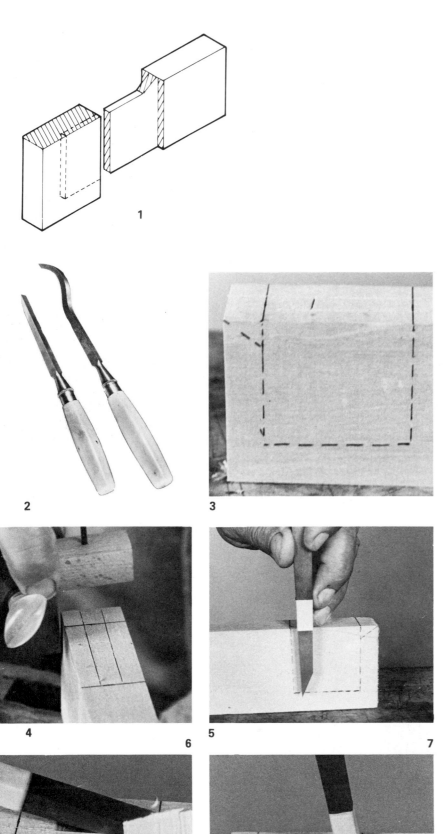

1

2

3

4

6

5

7

Chopping Mortises

In making any mortise-and-tenon joint, you should always make the mortise first and the tenon last. In this case we will chop out the mortise for a mitered haunched mortise and tenon **(1)**. The joint is completely hidden. Besides being hidden, this joint has the advantage of not needing a clamp across the cheeks. Because wood is left on the top of the mortise, the cheeks will be pulled in tight on their own. It is a good idea to keep the piece with the haunched mortise longer than you will need, to lessen the chance of it splitting when the pieces are glued up. You can cut off the excess after the pieces are glued together.

To chop out this mortise (or any mortise) with chisels, use a heavy-duty mortising chisel **(2-left)**. The steel is considerably thicker than that of a normal chisel. The chisel for making a ⅜-in. mortise is about ⅜ in. thick. The two sides are parallel, so once the chisel is started correctly it will guide itself to make a straight cut. The chisel can be used after holes have been drilled, to clean out the excess and square up the holes. I find, though, that the chisel works just as well without predrilling.

(2-right) The swan-neck chisel is like the heavy-duty mortise chisel, but the lower part is rounded to clean up the bottom of a mortise. Both chisels are sharpened like regular chisels, with the bevel at 30° (see p. 35).

(3) Locate the position of the mortise. (I'm using lines on the side for clarity). To set the width of the mortise, mark the board by hammering down the mortise chisel.

(4) Set the marking gauge to the width of the chisel mark and scribe.

(5) Mark the depth the mortise will be onto the chisel, using a piece of tape.

(6) Start to chisel out the center of the mortise. Work toward the edges until the chisel is down to the right depth.

(7) At the bottom of the mortise, undercut slightly to help ensure that the tenon will go in easily.

(8) Clean out the hole with the swan-neck chisel.

(9) Never use a chisel with your other hand in front of the tool, as demonstrated in this picture. Sooner or later, you are sure to cut yourself.

(10) After the mortise is cleaned out, the miter can be chiseled out and the mortise is finished.

(11) The tenon is marked with the marking gauge, and then cut with the bowsaw (see pp. 180-181).

I cut the cheeks of the tenon and the bevel before cutting the shoulders **(12)**.

(13) Now the joint is finished and is ready to assemble.

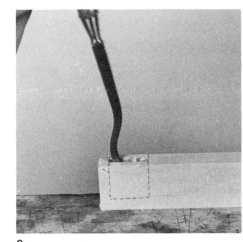

8

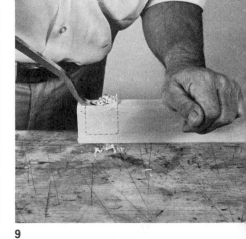

9

10

11

12

13

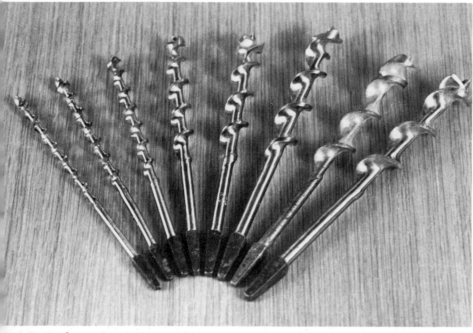

1

2

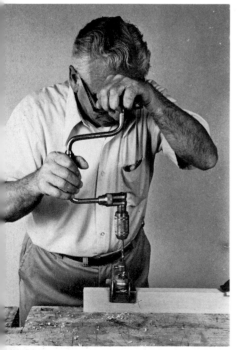

3

4

5

6

Drilling Mortises

Mortises can also be drilled out. I prefer auger bits **(1)** for hand-drilling. The drills come in different sizes. The center of an auger bit is longer than normal, and it is threaded to help pull the bit down. The other end is square to fit into the chuck of a brace. Auger bits will not fit into electric drills. Sometimes auger bits are hard to start in end grain. The end grain is often so hard that even the screwing action of the threaded end and the weight of your body are not enough to force the bit down. If that is the case, put a little water or spit at the start of the hole, and the wood will expand enough to give the thread a chance to grab.

(2) This is a brace. It is designed to hold drill and screwdriver bits. The smooth, round top handle spins easily. In this picture you can also see a piece of wood with a center hole drilled out. This is used as a depth stop (see p. 152). It is easy to make and doesn't mark up the surface of the wood the way steel stops often do.

(3) I use my head and hand to force the bit down. That is one time using my head comes in handy.

(4) When using any bit free-hand, mark the center of the mortise and the diameter of the bit. Drill the outside two holes first, to be sure to get clean, straight holes. If you try to drill the end holes after the center holes are drilled, the bit will tend to slide into the center holes, and you won't get a straight-sided mortise. Then continue drilling the rest of the holes. To control the depth, I use a piece of tape or a wooden stop like the one in picture **2**.

(5) A doweling jig can be used to guide the bit, but for some reason I cannot find a doweling jig and a set of auger bits in this country that fit together. I have tried sets manufactured by the same company, and was very frustrated when the auger would not fit into the corresponding bit guide. I finally gave up and made my own (see p. 170). Of course, an electric drill with a stop will do the job much faster.

(6) After all the holes are drilled to the right depth, mark the outside of the holes with a marking gauge.

(7,8) Use a wide chisel to clean the sides of the mortise.

(9,10) Then, using a chisel the same width as the bit, square the ends and clean the rest of the mortise. A heavy-duty mortise chisel and a swan-neck chisel of the right width could be used instead (see p. 166).

(11) A drill press can also be used for drilling mortises. In that case I would clamp a board to the table to act as a fence for the piece to slide against.

An attachment is available for most drill presses that holds a square hollow chisel. Or you can buy a mortiser **(12,13,14)**, a specialized machine designed solely to cut square holes. It uses a hollow chisel bit. The bed slides from right to left and moves backwards and forwards, and up and down, making positioning and cutting the mortise very simple.

With a square hollow chisel, the drill is in side and drills the hole while the chisel squares the hole. I have found these attachments to be fine for soft wood, and I mean soft wood. In hardwoods, the chisel has a tendency to get stuck in the first two outside holes. But after those are drilled, it is easy to drill the rest of the holes. □

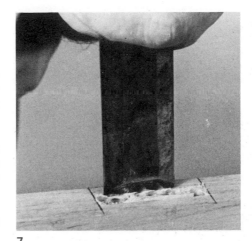

7

8

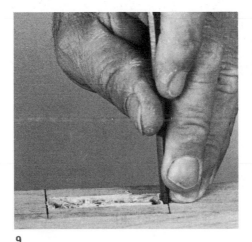

9

10

11

12

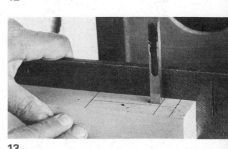

13

14

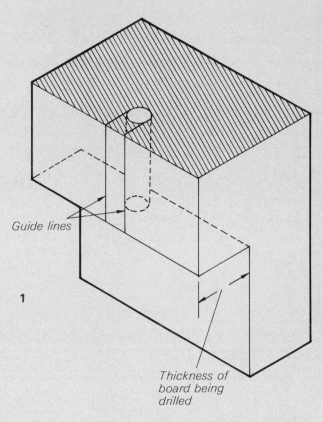

Guide lines

1

Thickness of board being drilled

Wooden Doweling Jig

The wooden doweling jig **(1)** is made from a piece of hardwood thicker than the piece you will be drilling into.

(2) Mark off the thickness of the piece that is to be drilled into.

(3) Then mark off a hole in the center and drill that hole through the end grain, using the same bit you plan to use to drill the mortise. If the hole is drilled by hand, it would be advisable to mark the center of the other end of the piece and drill halfway in from both ends.

(4) Then remove the area that is shaded.

(5) The diameter of the bit is marked on the outside of the block to locate the hole easily. The jig gets clamped to the piece **(6).** I find it works very well. □

2

3

6

4

5

Long-Hole Boring Machine

(1) A long-hole boring machine, or slot mortiser, is like a drill press lying on its side, so the drill is horizontal. Instead of a drill, use a long router bit. In front of the bit is a table that can move up and down, in and out and sideways. The piece that will receive the mortise is clamped down to this table. This machine is one of the fastest ways to mortise—much faster than with a hollow chisel bit. The only thing to watch with the long-hole borer is that if the hole is drilled too fast or forced to take off too much in one pass, the drill will whip, and the mortise sides will not be straight. Here again, drill the two outside holes first.

(2) Then move the table from side to side and in and out, slowly removing the excess between the holes, nearly the way you would if you were using a router. Here, though, the machine stays in place and the work is moved.

(3) The mortise is finished. This one will be used for a haunched mortise and tenon joint. □

1

2

3

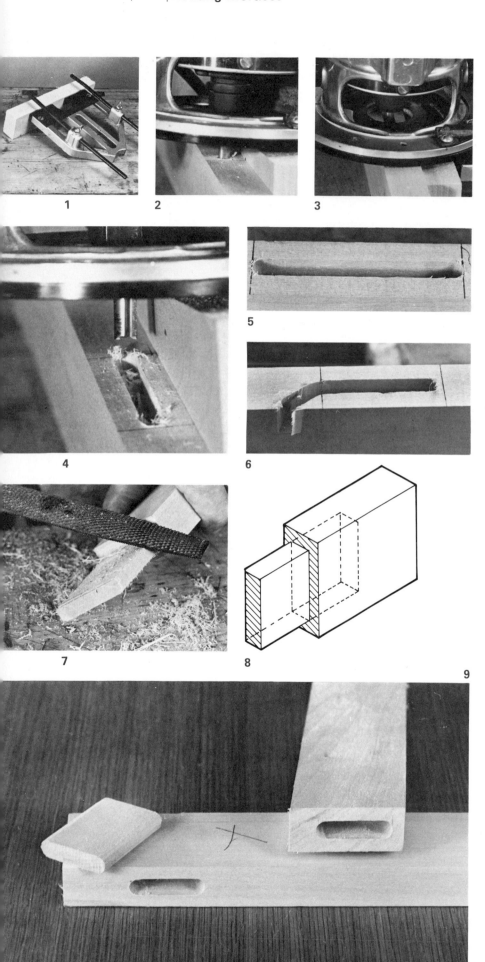

1

2

3

5

4

6

7

8

9

Routing Mortises

Routing is a fast and easy way to make a mortise if it does not have to be very deep. **(1)** Screw a piece of wood to the router fence. The piece has to be at least 1 in. wider than the length of the bit sticking out above the router plate. This way the fence can guide the router as the bit is dropped into the piece.

(2) Start the router and lower it down all the way. **(3)** With the fence tight up against the piece, slide the router until the whole mortise is made.

(4) Stop the router motor before lifting the bit out of the mortise.

(5) The mortise is much smoother than if made with a hollow chisel bit.

Be sure to move the router in the right direction so the bit is cutting in the mortise away from the fence. This will pull the fence tightly up against the piece being cut. If the router is moved in the opposite direction, the cutting action will be toward the fence, which will push the fence away from the piece. If you then try to force the fence against the piece, the router will be fighting you and the inside mortise will be very uneven. This picture **(6)** show what happens if the fence is not tight up against the piece. If you are not sure which direction to move the router in, try the router on a scrap piece. Don't push the fence all the way up against the piece. Move the router in both directions. In only one direction the fence will be pulled in up against the piece. This is the right direction. The router will tell you which way to move.

(7) The corners of the tenon can be rasped round, or the ends of the mortise can be squared with a chisel. I find rounding the tenon faster than squaring the mortise.

(8) If a tenon breaks, a spline can be inserted. The same method is often substituted for a mortise and tenon. It is not as strong, but in most cases is sufficient. It is much easier to make, especially with compound miters.

(9) Make the mortise in both pieces using a long-hole boring machine or router. Then fit the spline.   □

Making Tenons

Chapter 9

1

2

3

4

5

6

7

a   b

c

Half-Lap Joint, on a Table Saw

The safest way to make a half-lap joint on a table saw is to use a tenoning jig. The tenoning jig **(1)** is an attachment for the circular saw that fits into a groove in the top of the saw table normally used for the miter gauge. The upper plate that supports the work is 90° to the table, so that the work can run over the blade in a vertical position. On the right side of the jig, a screw or vise holds the piece to the upper plate. The position of the screw can be adjusted using a wrench, so that the screw clamps the wood in the center.

(2) The whole upper plate can be moved in and out from the sawblade to position the piece correctly for the cut. It will always be parallel to the sawblade.

To cut the half-lap joint, raise the sawblade to the width of the opposite piece to be joined. Set the tenoning jig so the blade cuts half the thickness of the piece, with the thickness of the sawblade on the waste side **(3)**. Make the cut for the cheek. Do the same for the second piece.

(4) With the cheeks cut, lower the sawblade to half the thickness of the piece. Remove the waste piece, using the miter gauge to push the work through.

(5) If you use the fence as a stop to guide placement of the cut, clamp a piece to the fence. Guide off this piece **(6)**, and you will control the length of the cut while preventing the cut-off piece from getting trapped between the blade and the fence and shooting back at you.

(7) This cutting method gives you a very clean, quick and accurate half-lap joint. □

Half-Lap Joint, with Router

(1) The half-lap joint can also be in the middle of a board.

(2) Set the router bit depth to half the thickness of the board to be joined. A ¼-in. straight bit is fine, although you could use a larger one, too. (You might notice that one side of the plate on my router is flat. I did not buy it that way. Once, I forgot to put some grooves in a cabinet, and I had to make them after the cabinet was glued together. Some of the grooves were close to the joining piece, so close that I had to remove the handle and cut a piece off the base so the router would fit in. Being a cheapskate, I never bought another base. But I have never missed the part I cut off in 20 years of using the router. It works just as well and serves as a good reminder.)

(3) Measure from the cutting edge of the bit to the edge of the router baseplate. In this case the distance is 2⅞ in., although the camera angle makes it appear 2¾ in.

(4) Mark the piece for the shoulder.

(5) From the shoulder, mark in toward the other end 2⅞ in., or whatever the distance you measured on your router, and **(6)** square the line across the piece.

(7) Clamp a piece of wood right on the line.

(8) Run the edge of the router plate against the clamped-on board, and make the first cut.

(9) If you made a router *T*-square for cutting tongue-and-groove joints (see p. 132), use that instead. This way, you have to mark only where the shoulder is, and set the *T*-square to the mark with the router cut in the waste side.

Clamp the square down and make the first cut. Now rout out the rest of the excess wood, starting at the end of the board so you don't cut out all the stock the router is riding on **(10)**. Repeat the process on all the pieces to be joined. When you finish, the pieces are ready to be glued together.

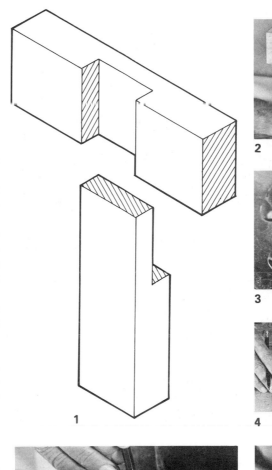

1

2

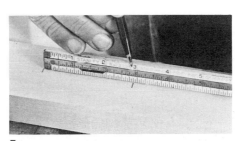

3

4

5

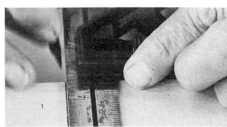

6

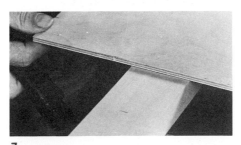

7

8

9

10

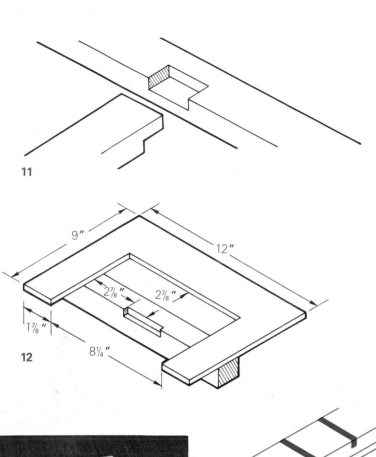

11

12

9"
12"
2⅞"
2⅞"
1⅞"
8¼"

13

14

15

16

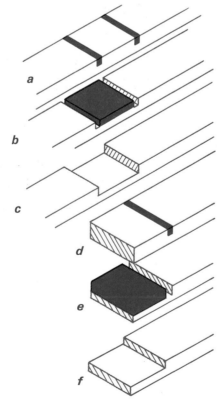

a

b

c

d

e

f

(11) If a piece has to join inside the frame for strength, a variation of the half-lap can be made.

(12,13) If you have several joints to make, it is worthwhile to build one of these jigs. The inside cut-out is the size of the joint plus 2⅞ in. more (or the distance from the cutting edge of the router bit to the edge of the base on your router) in each direction. Change these dimensions to fit your router-and-bit combination and the size joint you are working. This jig was made for the joint to go all the way across the width of the piece, but by moving out the piece of wood underneath the plywood, the joint can be made to go only partway in, as shown in drawing 11.

(14) Clamp the jig to the board and use the router, letting the base edges guide against both sides of the jig. Clean out the rest of the wood by moving the router back and forth **(15)**.

(16) One part of the half-lap is finished, and the jig is still on. ☐

Half-Lap Joint, with Router Plane

If you make half-lap joints by hand, begin by marking two lines where the pieces will intersect. Set the router plane to the depth of half the thickness of the board and draw the blade along both sides of the cut to mark the depth **(1)**.

(2) Saw the two outside cuts down to the halfway line, with the saw kerf on the waste side.

(3) To make it easier to chisel out the excess, I also saw an *X* in the center.

(4,5) Rough-chisel the waste wood out.

(6) For the final cut, use the router plane to even up the depth and make a smooth surface.

(7) The joint is finished.

1

2

3

4

5

6

7

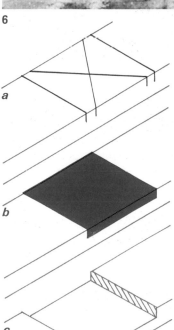

a

b

c

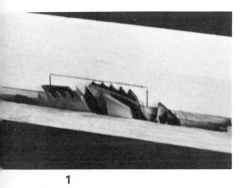

1

2

3

4

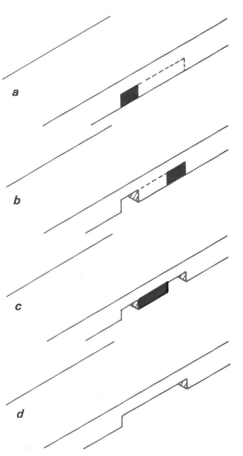

5

Half-Lap Joint, with Dado Head

A dado head can be used on the circular saw to make the half-lap joint. Set the height of the dado to exactly half the thickness of the wood **(1)**.

Mark the width of the cut. If many pieces are to be cut, use stops so all the widths are the same.

Make the two outside cuts first **(2)**.

(3) Then clean out the remaining wood, and **(4)** one piece is finished.

(5) The opposite part can also be made using a dado head. In this case, the dado head was not sharpened right. One of the spacers was longer than the other, causing ridges in the cut.   □

a

b

c

d

Half-Lap Joint, on the Band Saw

Use the widest blade the band saw can take, preferably at least ¾ in. wide.

(1) Clamp a board to the table to use as a fence. Set it for the distance of the cut of the cheek. Be sure the fence is parallel to the groove in the table and that it is square to the table. If the band saw has a fence attachment, you should of course use that.

(2) Clamp a stop for the back of the cut to the fence.

(3,4) Make the cheek cut.

(5) Using a miter gauge and a stop, make the shoulder cut and the joint is finished. This is a fast way to make the joint. The cut should be clean, but may not be as clean as if it were made on a circular saw.   □

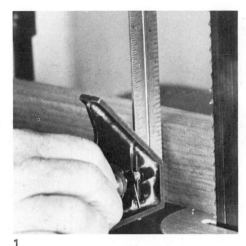

1

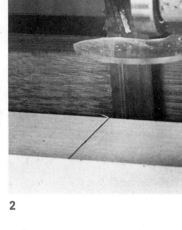

2

3

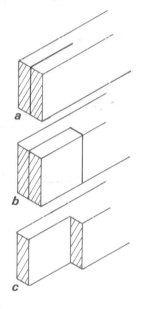

a

b

c

4

5

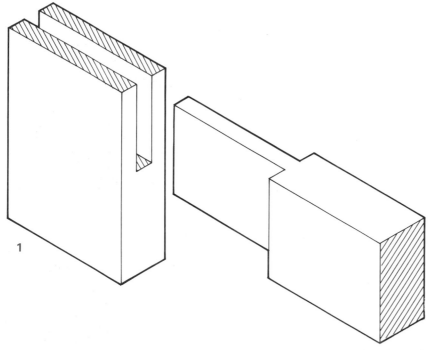

1

Slip Joint, with Bowsaw

The slip joint **(1)** is like a half-lap joint with two cheeks and two shoulders on each tenon piece. This doubles the glue surface and makes a very strong joint. The slip joint is easy to make, but like the half-lap, has the disadvantage of needing a lot of clamps to glue up correctly.

(2) When you glue together pieces that join in a slip joint you will have to clamp the joint in the direction of both the shoulders and the cheeks. So in a frame, you would need four clamps to get the shoulders tight, and four more to make sure the cheeks are clamped together. When you clamp the cheeks, use a block of wood under the clamp so you don't mar the pieces. It is advisable to put paper between the blocks and the frame so that the blocks are easier to remove if the glue should get underneath.

(3,4) Mark the two pieces on all four sides for the depth of the mortise and tenon. In a slip joint, this is the full width of the opposite joining part. Mark the face of the wood with an *X*, so that in laying out the joint, all pieces are marked from the same face. This ensures that the joints will go together perfectly, even if the two pieces differ slightly in thickness.

(5) Using a marking gauge, lay out the tenons on both edges and the ends of both pieces. Mark down to the line of the shoulders and the bottom of the tenon. You can also use a double marking gauge or two simple marking gauges at different settings. The important thing is to mark everything from the same face. Never mark from one face first and then from the back face. The same rule is good to follow when you use the circular saw. It is much more accurate to make two settings using the same face as reference than to turn the piece around and have only one setting.

Once the pieces are marked, clamp them in the vise at an angle. The trick to cutting accurate cheeks is to cut the back line and part of the top first, then turn the pieces around and use these cuts to guide the saw when making the final cuts **(6)**.

2

3

4

6

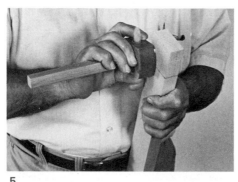

5

7

(7) The sawcut is on the waste side, just splitting the line in half. The piece to the right is the tenon, so the cuts are on the outside of the line. The piece to the left is the mortise, so the cuts are on the inside of the line.

(8) Turn the boards around and cut the rest of the top and front lines. Remember, leave the saw lying loosely in your hand and the saw will easily follow the sawcut in the back.

I have found a trick to improve the accuracy of the fit of the shoulders. This trick is especially useful for beginners. Essentially, you are making a small mini-shoulder for the saw to lean against. Scribe the line of the shoulders using a scratch awl **(9)**.

(10) Deepen the shoulder line by drawing the corner of a chisel along the line. The first pass should be very light, and more pressure should be applied successively in two or three more passes.

(11) Turn the chisel around and cut a second line at an angle, making a small half-V **(12)**.

(13) This V serves as a guide for the saw.

(14) Chisel out the center cut for the mortise from both sides. Undercut slightly, as in making dovetails.

(15) The joint is ready to glue together. I was lucky again—it fit perfectly.   □

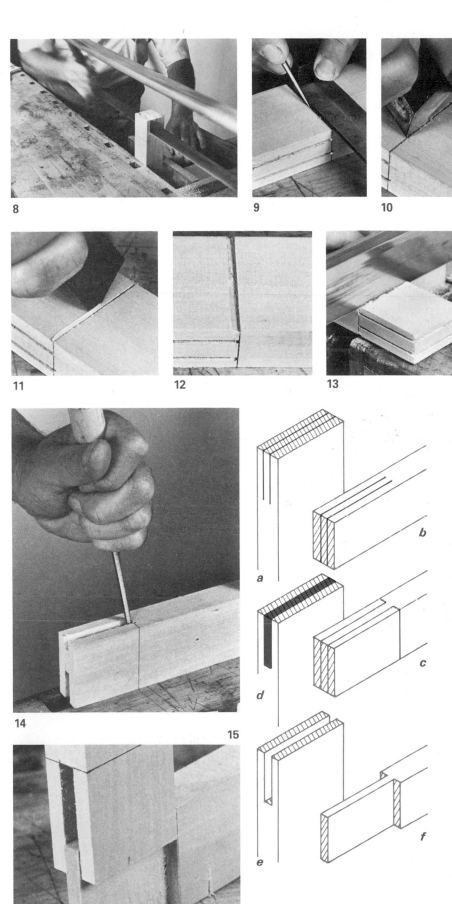

8

9

10

11

12

13

14

15

a

b

c

d

e

f

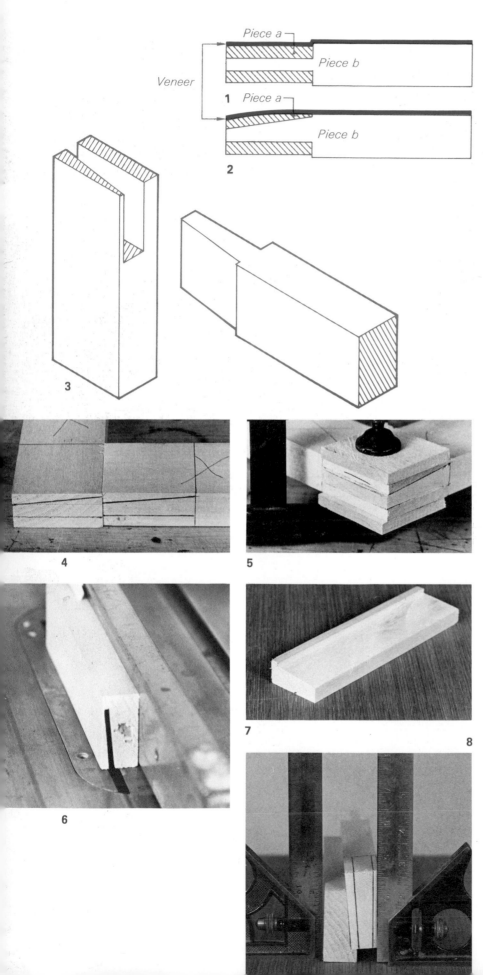

Tapered Slip Joint

Wood moves differently, depending on what part of the tree it comes from. In a slip joint **(1)**, pieces a and b will move differently. If veneer is applied to the face of this joint, the differences in expansion and contraction will cause the joint eventually to telegraph through the veneer, showing a sharp line.

(2,3) By using the tapered slip joint shown here, telegraphing will be minimized. The difference in movement is reduced where the thin edge of the mortise meets with the shoulder, and the difference will appear as a slight curve rather than a sharp line on the veneer.

(4) A tapered slip joint that will be veneered over is laid out as in this picture.

(5) Here is the joint glued together. If I had only a few frames to make, I would cut the joints by hand with a bowsaw exactly as when making a regular slip joint (see p. 180).

If you want to make this joint by machine, use a table saw. Tilt the blade to the desired angle for the tenon, and make a jig out of wood to hold the mortise pieces at an angle for the cut **(6,7)**. The jig angle is the same as for the angles of the mortise.

(8) Here the piece is inserted in the jig.

To hold the wood for making the cuts, I find it easiest to use the jig made for cutting tongue-and-groove joints (see p. 131). Or use the tenoning jig. **(9)** Clamp the tapered jig and the piece to be cut to the jig that sits over the fence.

(10,11) With the blade vertical and the tenoning jig in place, cut the tapered mortise first, with the piece clamped to the tapered jig.

Then without the tapered jig, cut the other side of the mortise.

(12) Now cut the tapered cheek of the tenon with the blade at an angle.

Change the blade back to vertical, cut the other cheek of the tenon, and then the two shoulder cuts (as described in the section on half-lap joints — see p. 174). ☐

9

10

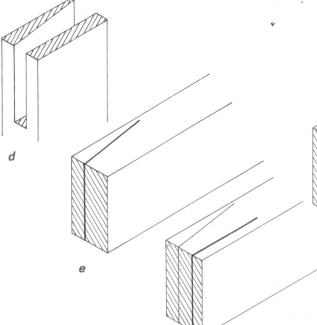

11

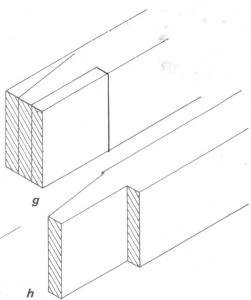

12

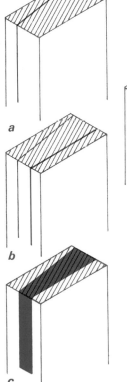

a

b

c

d

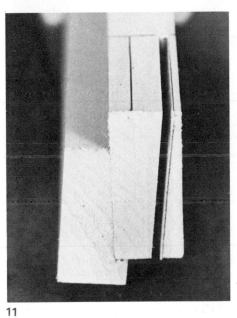

e

f

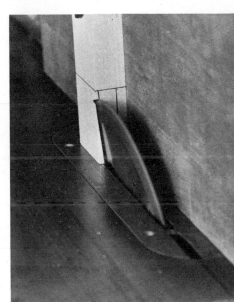

g

h

1

Tenons, with Miter Saw and Plane-Iron Jig

A fast and easy way to make small tenons by hand is to use a miter box and saw, and a special jig that consists of a block of wood with a hole in it, a plane iron, a screw, and two small blocks of wood.

(1) A miter saw is a large backsaw that is inserted into a guide in the front and the back. The saw can be set to make cuts at different angles. The table and the back fence are square. To hold the piece of wood firmly, the face of the table is a little bit rough. There is a stop that can be set for any length cut. The depth of the cut is controlled by setting the saw so that it cannot cut below a certain point. Each miter box works a little differently. How to set and operate each type is described thoroughly in the pamphlet that comes with the saw. If you get a used saw and there are no instructions, try out the adjustments and it will become obvious which knob or screw adjusts which setting.

(2,3) Using the depth stops, set the saw to make the right depth cuts for the shoulders.

(4) Set the stop for the correct length.

(5) Cut all the shoulders. Now we are ready to use the plane-iron jig (see p. 186).

(6) Clamp the jig to the bench with the hole to the outside so the waste can fall through. Set the blade to the right position.

(7) Secure the blade by tightening the screw. For fine adjusting, the screw can be tightened a little more and the blade will bend slightly. Don't tighten it too much.

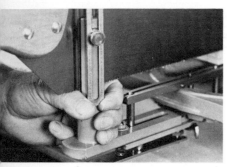

2

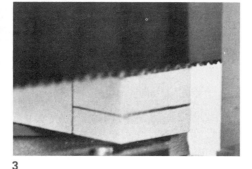

3

4

5

6

7

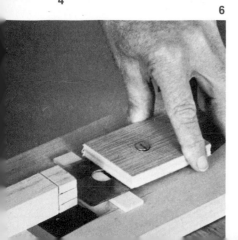

Hold the piece with the tenon down against the jig and hit the back end with a wooden mallet **(8,9)**.

(10) The cheek is cut.

(11) Do the same on the other side, and the tenon is finished.

This is the safest way to make a tenon by hand. However, the grain in the tenon has to be straight or it might not cut cleanly. I use this jig only on small tenons, and usually where a lot of pieces have to be inserted close together, such as in a gate. It is surprising how well the tenons come out. If you use this system, I would advise making a couple of extra pieces in case one or two of the tenons don't work out.   □

8

9

10

11

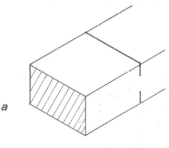

a

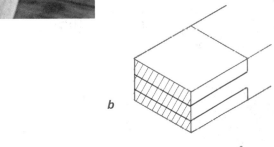

b

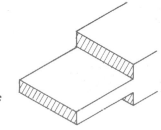

c

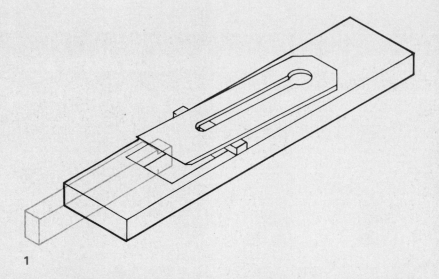

1

2

3

Plane-Iron Jig

The plane-iron jig **(1)** is used to cut tenons quickly.

(2) Here the plane-iron jig is disassembled. The large hole allows the waste to fall through. The block that goes across is movable and controls the height of the blade (and therefore the cut). When the screw is tightened, the block with the hole prevents the blade from moving.

(3) A *T*-nut is inserted in the bottom of the jig. A *T*-nut has a threaded hole and sharp metal points that can be hammered into a piece of wood and will stay in place.

(4,5) *T*-nuts come in a variety of screw and thread sizes, and are used frequently in furniture that is meant to disassemble easily.

(6) Here the jig is assembled.   □

4

5

6

Tenons on a Table Saw, Using Two Blades

The tenon is made exactly like the half-lap joint (see p. 174), but two settings have to be made because there are two cheeks and shoulders. Always make the mortise first.

To cut a tenon on the circular saw with only one blade and a tenoning jig (see p. 174), make the first cut **(1)**, then reset for the second cut **(2)**. Don't flip the wood around, because there might be a difference in the thickness.

(3) An easier way to cut tenons on the circular saw is to use two sawblades of exactly the same diameter. Make washers the same size as the different tenons you need, corresponding with the bit you use to make the mortises. These washers can be made out of steel, aluminum or wood. If you use wood, be sure the two blades clamp up against end grain so humidity will not change the thickness of the washer.

(4) Put both blades on the arbor with the washers in between.

(5) Clamp the wood in the tenoning jig and make both cheek cuts at the same time. Then cut the shoulders as described in half-lap joints. □

2

3

1

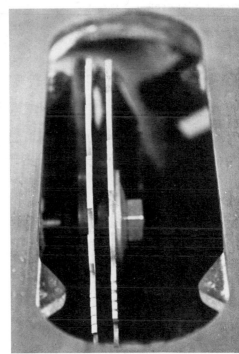

4

a

b

c

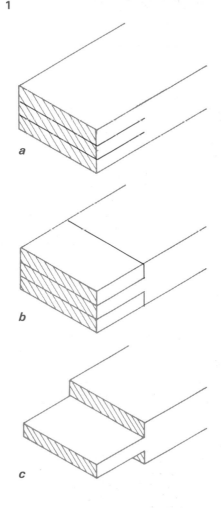

5

1

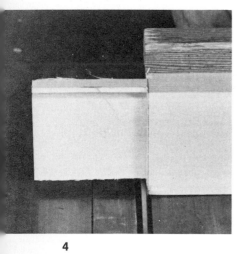

4

5

6

7

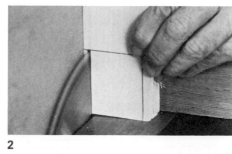

2

3

a

b

c

d

e

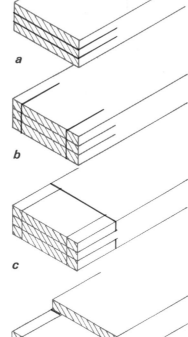

Tenons on a Table Saw, Using One Blade

A fast way to make tenons, which I have been using for years, is to use the fence instead of the tenoning jig. This technique is not nearly as safe, and I would not recommend it for beginners. Wait until you are familiar with the circular saw. Don't use pieces that are too wide, and use only one sawblade.

(1) Screw a piece of plywood to the fence that is wide enough so your hands will be above the blade. Then cut the cheeks. Here I am making a four-shouldered joint.

(2,3) With two cheeks cut, I make the other two vertical cuts. For safety, I use a miter gauge behind the piece.

(4) Then I cut the four shoulders. Use a stop as for half-lap joints (see p. 174) to ensure that all four shoulders are precisely in the same plane **(5)**.

(6) I have an old Danish machine for cutting tenons. I am sorry to say it isn't available any more. It has two knives, a track that is bolted to the table on which a sleigh slides, and a clamp that holds the wood down.

(7) With the piece of wood secured and the shaper turned on, the sleigh is pushed forward. A spacer between the knives allows both cheeks and both shoulders to be cut in one sweep. With a little engineering, a track and a sleigh could be designed to fit any shaper. For small production, it would be worthwhile to invest the money, because so much time is saved making tenons this way. □

Tenons at an Angle

(1) In a chair, the back is usually 1 in. or 2 in. narrower than the front. This is done more for appearance than for any other reason. This means the sides will angle into the back. Usually the angle is in the tenon—it is easier to make an angled tenon than an angled mortise. There is a limit to how much a tenon can be angled. As long as some long grain reaches the full length of the tenon, it is strong enough. (In critical cases you can angle the mortise, but that is much more difficult. I would make a special jig to hold the stock at an angle for the router or mortising machine.)

Making an angled tenon is just as easy as making a straight tenon. **(2)** Tilt the two blades to the correct angle and make the cut as if it were straight. If you use only one blade, set both cuts from the same side of the board and lower the blade for the lower cut.

To cut the shoulders, if using two sawblades, remove one sawblade and the washer. Leave the blade at the same angle as when cutting the cheeks. Set the blade to the right height, and using the miter gauge, make the shoulder cut **(3)**, which is perpendicular to the cheek.

(4) For the other shoulder, keep the same blade tilt, but lower the blade. Move the miter gauge to the opposite slot in the table. Set the piece so the blade is exactly in line with the other shoulder. Then make the cut. ☐

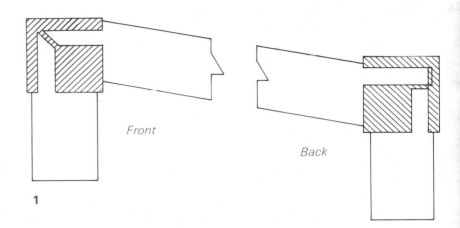

Front

Back

1

2

3

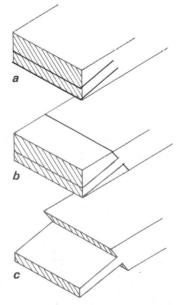

a

b

c

4

1

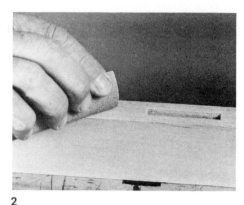

2

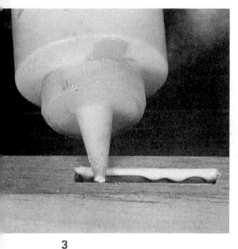

3

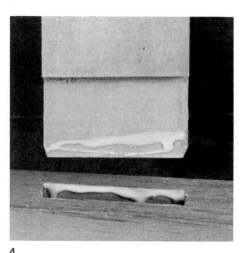

4

Assembling a Mortise and Tenon

(1) To make the joint easier to assemble, cut the corner in the width of the tenon.

To test the fit of the tenon, push it in the mortise by hand, using only the weight of your body to force it in. If you have to use a hammer, the tenon is too tight and the mortise could split. If the tenon is too loose, glue a piece of veneer or a thin piece of wood to one or both cheeks and saw it again on the table saw. If you make the cut with a bowsaw, you will need a thicker piece of wood so the thickness of the blade is secured on both sides.

(2) Remember always to plane and sand the inside edges of the frame before gluing it together. It'll be much more difficult afterwards.

(3) When gluing, put the glue in the mortise, especially on the top edges. When the tenon slides into the mortise it will push the glue ahead of it.

(4) I also put a little glue on the end of the tenon. The glue will be pushed up as the tenon slides in. Don't put too much glue on either piece or it will be all over the bench, the floor and you. And the excess glue will be forced up to the surface and could split the joint. ☐

Mitered Frame Joints

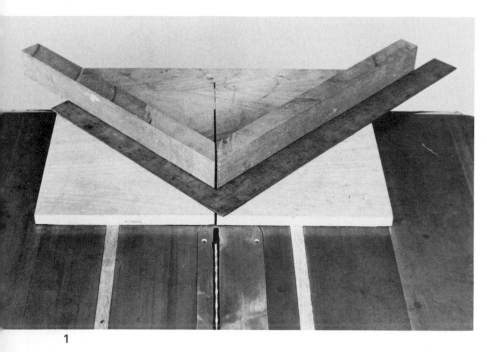

Chapter 10

1

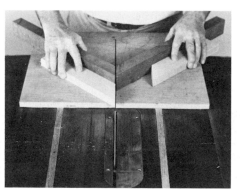

2   3

4

Jig for Cutting Miters

A fast and accurate way to cut a 45° corner is on the circular saw. A special jig **(1)** makes the procedure easy and foolproof. The jig is made exactly like the jig for cutting square cut-offs (see p. 43). Fit two pieces into the grooves in the top of the saw table, and screw and glue them underneath a piece of plywood. Then make a cut halfway through, and attach a piece of hardwood at exactly 45° to the cut. Then fasten on another piece of hardwood, mitered square to the first piece. Check the angle with a square.

(2) Make sure that the two pieces are also square to the surface of the plywood.

When you use the jig, always cut one piece on one side of the jig **(3)**, and the mating piece on the other **(4)**. This way, you can be sure the two will come out square. ☐

Frame Spline Miters

There are several ways to make a mitered frame joint. A strong and easy way is with an exposed spline **(1)**.

(2) Cut the miters and apply hot glue to the edges. Make sure the glue isn't too thin.

(3) Put a piece of paper under the joint. Rub the two surfaces together while the glue is still hot. Work fast and rub hard so that all the excess glue gets squeezed out. Stop, rubbing as soon as the excess is squeezed out and the glue is cold. The joint will stay together. You won't need to use any clamps. After an hour or two the joint will be strong enough for cutting the spline.

(4,5) A jig holds the mitered pieces while you cut out the spline slots. This piece should be fairly wide to get a large enough 90° section cut out of it. Use a handsaw or band saw.

(6) Put the jig against the fence. Raise the sawblade as high as it will go without coming through the inside of the joint.

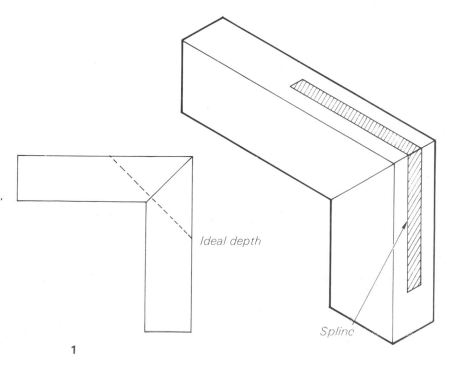

Ideal depth

Spline

1

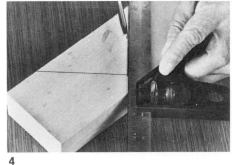

2

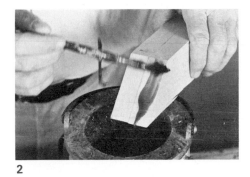

3

4

5

6

7

8

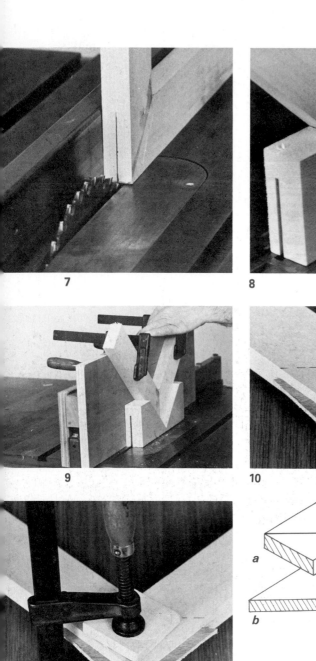

9

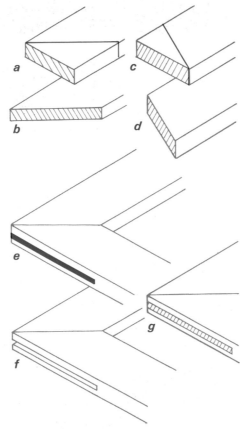

10

11

12

(7) Set the fence so the blade will cut through the center of the frame. (Sometimes you may wish to use more than one spline.) Or if you need a thicker spline, use a dado head to cut the slot.

(8) Hold the mitered piece down firmly in the jig, and push the jig through the blade. The spline slot will be cut into the mitered piece.

(9) A safer but more time-consuming way to hold the piece is to clamp the jig to the over-the-fence tenoning jig used for tongue-and-groove joints (see p. 131).

(10) Once the kerf is made, fit a piece for the spline and glue it in, with the grain running across the cut. Make splines on a circular saw or by putting them through a thickness planer (with a board underneath if they are less than ¼ in. thick).

(11) I would advise that you clamp the spline in to get a tight joint.

(12) The joint is finished. Contrasting wood splines make it decorative. In a thick piece, several splines can be used.   □

Miter Box

A miter box with a saw is costly. You can make an inexpensive box **(1)** out of ¾-in. or 1-in. stock that will work just as well. Make the side pieces about 3 in. wide, and the bottom 5 in. wide. Be sure the bottom is the same width throughout its length (so the sides will sit parallel) and that the sides are the same height throughout, too.

(2) Attach the side pieces a little lower than the bottom, so that the box will be more stable. Once the side pieces are aligned, glue and nail them on.

(3) The side pieces must be square to the bottom.

For the square saw slot in the box, draw a square line across the top and down both side pieces. For the 45° cut, measure the width of the box (in this case, 6½ in.). Mark off a distance that is exactly the same as the width measurement. Square the lines across at each end. **(4)** Draw lines between the two outside points of the square on each diagonal.

(5) Once everything is marked, cut the angled saw slot. Hold the saw so that it matches the point on the back piece and the line down the front side simultaneously. Finish the sawcut the opposite way, and you will have a perfect cut. This is essentially the same method used to make tenons by hand (see pp. 180-181).

(6) If the box is to be used along with the plane-iron jig for slicing tenon shoulders, place a piece of wood in the bottom of the box of the right thickness to control the depth of the cut, and clamp a block of wood at the right distance to make a stop for the correct length. □

(Same as width of box)

6½"

3"

6½"

2'

1

2

3

4

5

6

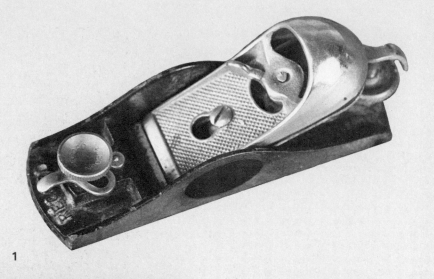

1

2

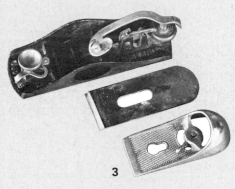

3

Block Plane

The block plane **(1)** is designed to plane end grain.

The screw in the front of the plane adjusts the slot in the front **(2)** where the shavings come through.

The plane adjusts and the iron is secured exactly like any other steel plane, but there is no chipbreaker, and the blade is actually inserted upside down with the bevel facing up **(3)**. Also, the blade is tilted at a much smaller angle.

If a joint is not perfect **(4)**, you can straighten it out with a block plane.

(5,6) With the wood secured in a vise, the surface is planed smooth and the angle corrected. The block plane works better if held at an angle.

(7) The joint is corrected and ready to be glued. □

4

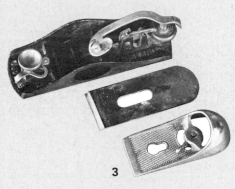

5

6

7

Hidden Spline Miter, on a Table Saw

(1) The spline miter can also be hidden from the outside but exposed on the inside.

(2,3) Cut the slot with a dado head or saw-blade and the tenoning jig with a stop (see p. 174).

With the piece clamped to the jig, push the jig to the stop and one cut is made **(4)**. Here the spline must be exactly in the center because the two pieces are clamped to the jig from opposite faces.

(5) Both cuts are made and are ready for the spline. Because the cut does not go all the way through on the outside, the cut will be rounded at the end. The end of the spline will have to be cut round to fit.

(6) The spline is fitted in the joint and **(7)** the joint is ready to be glued. This joint could also be made using a router.   ☐

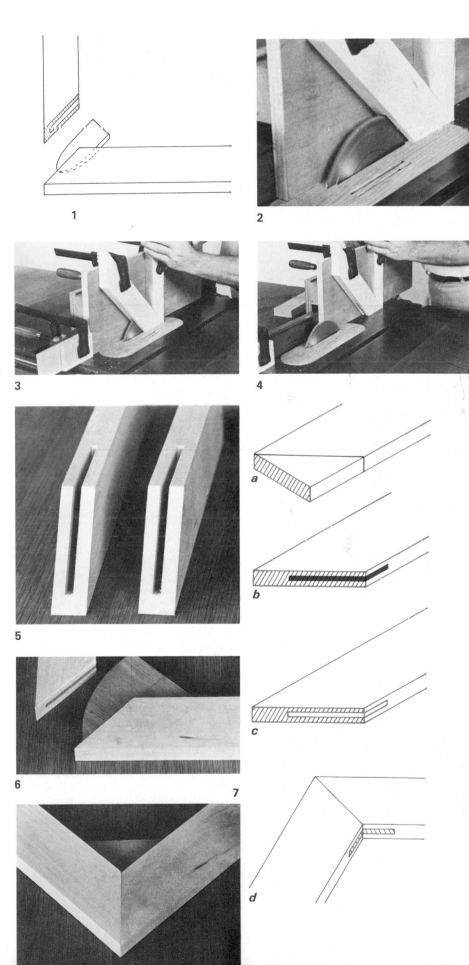

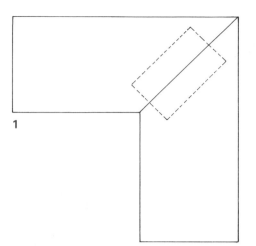

1

2

3

Hidden Spline Miter, with a Router

(1) Another quite strong miter can be made that is completely hidden from both sides. It is quick and easy to make using the long-hole boring machine or a router, which I am using here.

(2) When the miters are cut, rout a slot in each mitered piece using the wooden fence as a guide, exactly as if making mortises. The router bit may wander when first inserted into the wood, as in the piece on the left in picture 3. To avoid this, raise the bit up beyond the plate, place the router on the piece to be cut, start it and then lower the bit to the desired depth. Then rout out the slot, stop the router and remove it. The drawback to this method is that it takes two people. Cut from the same face on both pieces.

(3) Make a spline to fit, and **(4)** the joint is ready to go together. ☐

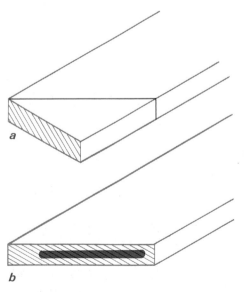

a

b

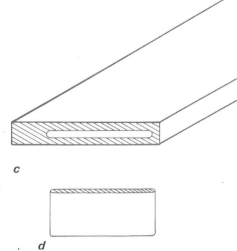

c

d

4

Hidden Mitered Mortise and Tenon

To make a hidden mitered mortise-and-tenon joint **(1)**, miter the ends of both pieces that will be joined.

Make the mortise by one of the methods described earlier (see pp. 166-172).

(2) Clamp the tenon piece to the jig that rides over the fence, or use the tenoning jig that can be purchased for the saw. Be sure the 45° surface rests tightly on the saw table. After the cheeks are cut, cut the shoulders.

(3) Mark the tenon to the right length so it fits the mortise.

(4) Cut off the excess, and the joint is ready to assemble.

(5) The mortise-and-tenon construction is hidden on the finished miter.   □

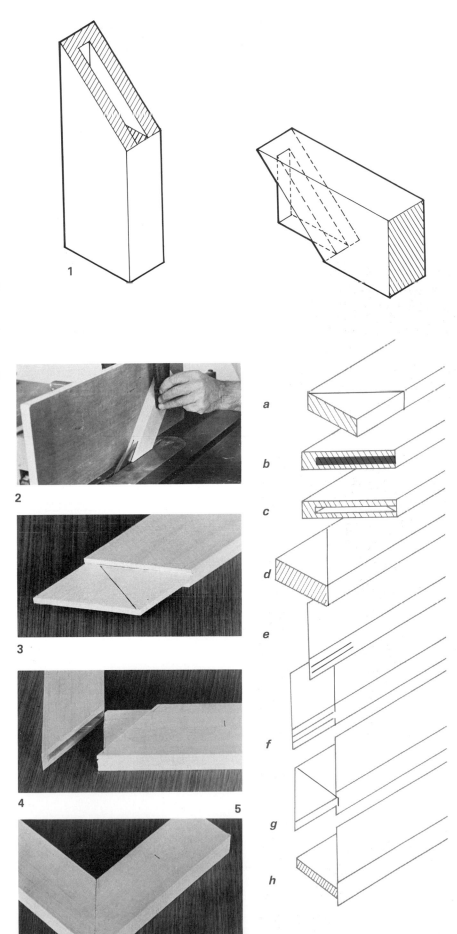

1

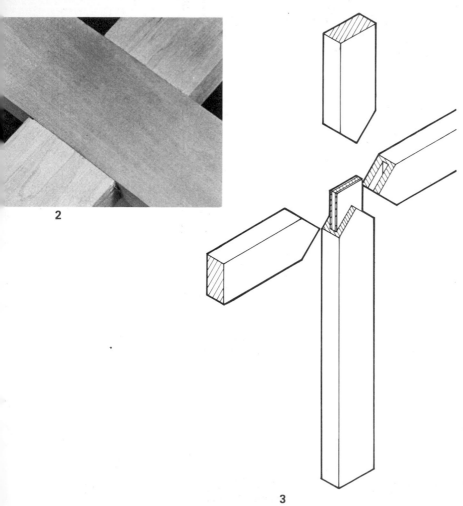

2

Joint Where Two Pieces Cross

If you are making a joint where both pieces meet in the center, as in a cross, a half-lap joint might not look very good. **(1)** Here, for example, the striped lines match, and a half-lap joint **(2)** would ruin the effect.

To make the joint **(3)** cut the four pieces 45° from both sides **(4,5)**.

3

Be sure the point is exactly centered in the width of the wood **(6)**.

(7) Clamp the pieces in the *V*-cut jig that slides along the fence (see p. 193).

(0) Slice the piece for a spline the same way as when adding a spline to a 45° butt-jointed frame (see p. 194).

(9) When all four pieces are cut, insert a plywood spline, and glue and clamp the pieces together.

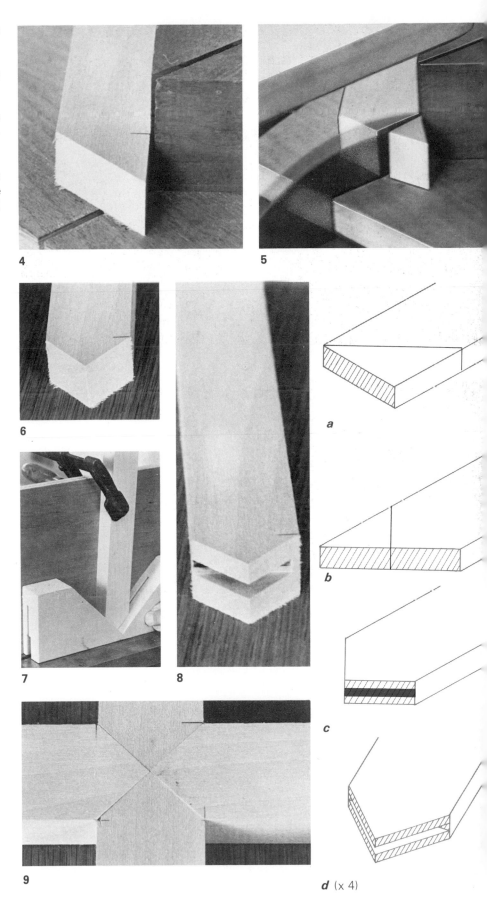

4

5

6

7

8

a

b

c

9

d (x 4)

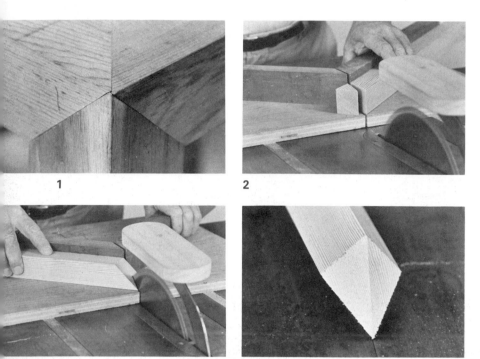

1

2

3

4

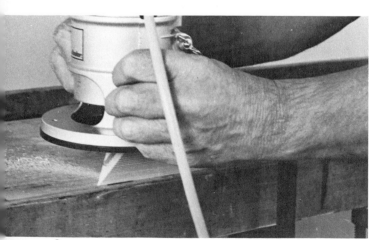

5

6

Three-Way Miter, at End

A three-way 45° joint where three pieces meet at right angles **(1)** is very difficult to make. But it is useful for making parsons tables and the like. All the pieces have to be exactly square and the same size and thickness. The circular saw blade must be square to the table, and the 45° miter gauge setting or jig must be accurate. I suggest that you make a full-scale drawing of the side and front view of the piece to refer to for your exact measurements. I made a small table here to show how the joint is glued together, and I had one of those days. I goofed up one piece three times and the table got smaller and smaller. So if it doesn't work for you the first time, don't feel bad.

If the pieces are to meet at the end, cut all three pieces alike. **(2)** Cut the ends to 45°.

(3) For the second cut, turn the piece so the first 45° cut faces up.

When you set a stop for the second cut, make sure that the cut is made so that it meets exactly with the corner of the square piece **(4)**.

Cut all the pieces the same way. Then use a router with a jig **(5,6)** like the one for making multiple spline miters (see p. 112)—but here there is only one slot on each angled face. If you have a long-hole boring machine or a mortiser, you can cut the slots more easily and precisely.

(7,8) Chisel the corners square and make the splines.

(9) The joint is finished and ready to glue.

(10) I finally got lucky and made that joint fit. A web clamp covers part of the joint. □

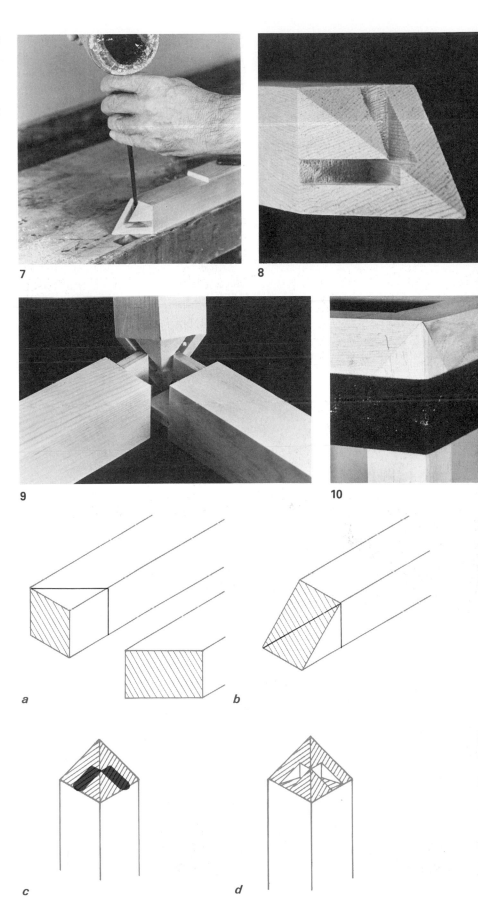

7

8

9

10

a

b

c

d

1

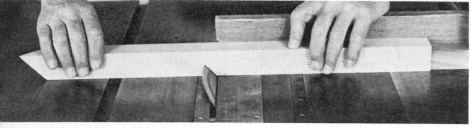

2

3

4

5

6

Three-Way Miter, in Middle

When three pieces meet at right angles but not at the end of the pieces, the three-way miter joint is considerably harder to make. A lot more machine setup is involved.

(1) If you are using a three-way joint at both the end and at the center, make sure you position the second joint so the piece will go in the same direction as on the top joint.

Tilt the sawblade to 45° and set it to the right height so the bottom of the *V*-cut is precisely in the middle of the piece. Be sure the miter gauge is at 90°. Then make the first two cuts **(2,3)**.

Turn the piece around, put a stop on (clamped to the fence), and make the next two cuts **(4,5)**.

Then make the mortises in the cuts for the splines. **(6)** So the two pieces will fit the joint mate, make them as for the joint where two pieces cross (see p. 200).

(7,8) Because the two pieces have to meet in the corner, the insides of the pieces also have to be cut to 45°.

(9,10) The joint is ready to be glued.   □

7

8

9

10

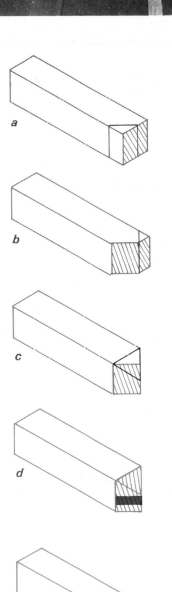

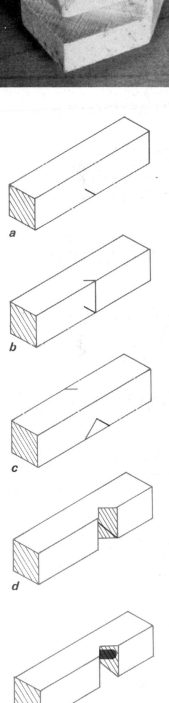

1

2

3

Gluing Up a Three-Way Miter

If you make a table that uses three-way miter joints, gluing up can be a very difficult task. It's less hectic to do it in two stages.

(1) First glue up the joints that are not on the ends. (In this table, these joints are in the lower apron.) Use a strap or band clamp to pull the pieces in snugly. The other joint (here the upper apron) has to be clamped, too, but should not be glued. Check the table for squareness.

(2) When the glue is dry, the other joint can be glued, using a strap clamp and bar clamps. Again, check for squareness.

(3) If you have help and can work fast, the whole table could be glued in one shot, but I wouldn't recommend trying it. ☐